MAYER SMITH

Billionaire in Hiding

Contents

1 The Fall from Grace · 1
2 Escape to Nowhere · 7
3 A Job and a New Life · 15
4 Clash of Personalities · 23
5 Small Town, Big Secrets · 31
6 A Glimpse of the Past · 40
7 The Past Never Forgets · 49
8 Shadows of the Past · 57
9 The Deal · 65
10 Breaking Point · 73
11 The Calm Before the Storm · 80
12 The Gathering Storm · 88
13 Unraveling the Lies · 95
14 The Reckoning · 103
15 Tipping the Scales · 110
16 The Final Hour · 117
17 The Last Stand · 124
18 The Final Hour · 131
19 Aftermath · 139
20 New Beginnings · 146

One

The Fall from Grace

The neon lights of the Manhattan skyline flickered against the darkened glass of Ethan Cole's penthouse, casting long, fractured reflections over the pristine marble floors. His whiskey glass trembled in his hand as he stared at the massive screen on the opposite wall, the volume low but the voices sharp enough to slice through his composure.

"Breaking news: Billionaire mogul Ethan Cole is at the center of a financial scandal that has rocked the business world. Allegations of fraud and corporate mismanagement have surfaced, sending his company's stock into a freefall. Cole himself has not been seen since the accusations went public, leaving many to wonder—where is Ethan Cole?"

The camera cut to a swarm of reporters outside Cole Enterprises, microphones thrust forward, faces hungry for a statement that would never come. Then, an image of him appeared—one from just weeks ago at a high-profile gala, suited in the finest Italian fabric, a glass of champagne in one hand, his signature confident smirk in place.

That was before.

Now, his life was crumbling around him, and he was standing in the wreckage.

His phone vibrated violently on the counter. Another call. He didn't need to look at the screen to know who it was. They all wanted the same thing—answers. From his board members, his lawyers, his so-called friends, even the people who once worshipped him but now only sought to dissect him like vultures over a carcass.

Ethan ran a hand through his disheveled dark hair, his jaw clenched. He had spent years building his empire from the ground up, clawing his way into the upper echelons of wealth and power. And now, in the span of seventy-two hours, it had all been snatched away, twisted by lies, deceit, and a scandal that wasn't even entirely his fault.

His CFO, Patrick Vaughn, had been the mastermind behind the shady financial dealings, but when the investigation began, Vaughn had vanished, leaving Ethan holding the bag. The evidence—conveniently manipulated—pointed straight to him. He could fight it. He could stand before the world and plead his case. But deep down, he knew it wouldn't matter.

The public had already made up their minds. Ethan Cole was guilty.

A pounding at the door shattered his thoughts.

"Ethan! Open the damn door!"

His best friend and attorney, Graham Lockwood, was on the other side, his voice strained with urgency. Ethan exhaled sharply, set his glass down, and strode toward the door, unlocking it with a practiced swipe of his hand. Graham pushed inside before it had fully opened, his sharp blue eyes scanning the apartment like a man expecting to find a dead body.

"Jesus, Ethan." He dragged a hand through his already-messy blond hair. "Have you been watching the news? They're tearing you apart."

Ethan gave him a dry look. "I noticed."

Graham swore under his breath. "The Feds are going to come after you hard. Your accounts are frozen, the board is calling for your resignation, and investors are pulling out like rats from a sinking ship. You need a plan."

Ethan walked back toward the floor-to-ceiling windows, looking down at the city. A city that once bowed to him, that once hung on his every word. Now, it was ready to spit him out.

"There is no plan," he said flatly. "They've already decided I'm guilty. It doesn't matter what I do."

"Like hell it doesn't." Graham marched toward him. "Listen to me, Ethan. You have two options. You can stay here, let them arrest you, let the media chew you up, and hope your lawyers can clear your name before they destroy you completely. Or…"

Ethan turned to face him, sensing the weight in his friend's pause. "Or what?"

"Disappear."

Ethan's brows lifted slightly, but he wasn't entirely surprised. Graham was nothing if not strategic.

"You want me to run?"

"I want you to be smart." Graham stepped closer, lowering his voice as if the walls had ears. "You know how this game is played. Perception is reality. The longer you're in the spotlight, the worse this gets. Right now, they see you as an arrogant billionaire who thought he could get away with it. But if you vanish? If you fall off the grid? Suddenly, you're a mystery. Suddenly, people start wondering if maybe they were wrong about you."

Ethan exhaled, rolling his shoulders as tension built at the base of his neck. The thought of running—of leaving everything he had built—made his stomach turn. But what choice did he have? Stay and let the wolves rip him apart? Or vanish, at least until he could clear his name?

"Where the hell would I even go?" he asked.

Graham smirked. "I've got a place in mind. A little nowhere town in the middle of the country. No cameras, no press, no one who gives a damn about billionaires. Just working-class people who mind their own business."

Ethan crossed his arms. "And what, I'm supposed to just pretend to be some regular guy?"

Graham's smirk widened. "You always said you wanted to know what life was like outside of penthouses and private jets. Consider this your chance."

Ethan's jaw tensed. He hated how much sense it made.

A sudden explosion of noise from outside made both men snap their heads toward the windows. Flashing lights. Sirens. Movement.

Ethan's stomach dropped.

"They're here," Graham muttered, stepping back. "If you're doing this, we have about sixty seconds before they knock down that door."

His pulse hammered against his ribs. He had spent his life in control. Calling the shots. Now, for the first time, he had no power. No way to turn this in his favor.

A sharp, decisive breath passed through his lips.

"Tell me what I need to do."

Graham grinned. "Now you're thinking like a survivor."

In the next thirty seconds, Ethan grabbed a duffel bag, stuffing it with essentials. Graham handed him a fake ID, cash, and a set of keys.

"New name, new life. You're Ethan Carter now. Hop on a train, head west, and don't look back."

Ethan met his friend's gaze, a rare flicker of gratitude in his usually unreadable eyes. "I owe you."

Graham smirked. "Damn right you do. Now go."

With one last glance around his penthouse—the last reminder of the life he was leaving behind—Ethan slipped out the back entrance just as the front door burst open with a crash.

As he disappeared into the night, the echoes of the past faded behind him.

And the world was left wondering where Ethan Cole had gone.

Two

Escape to Nowhere

The rhythmic clatter of train tracks beneath him was the only sound Ethan could focus on. He sat in the back corner of the near-empty passenger car, his hood pulled low over his face, the brim of his baseball cap casting a shadow that hid his sharp features. The stale scent of recycled air and cheap coffee from the cart attendant filled his nose, a stark contrast to the expensive colognes and polished leather of his usual world.

He was officially gone.

Ethan Cole no longer existed. Now, he was Ethan Carter, a nobody with no past, no future, and no direction.

The train rocked gently as it cut through the darkness, leaving New York City—and everything that came with it—far behind.

Outside, the view had transformed from towering skyscrapers to endless fields, a vast nothingness stretching as far as the eye could see. It had been hours since they'd last stopped at any place of significance, and now, all that remained were forgotten stations, run-down platforms, and the occasional cluster of dimly lit buildings.

Ethan tapped his fingers against the armrest, his thoughts spiraling.

The plan was simple: disappear. Lay low until he figured out his next move. Graham had given him this destination—a tiny, middle-of-nowhere town called Willow Creek, where no one knew his name, and, more importantly, no one cared. He'd stay out of sight, live off the cash Graham had given him, and avoid anything that could get him recognized.

But despite the plan, a tight knot had formed in his chest.

He wasn't used to this. He wasn't used to not being in control.

His entire life had been built on precision, on power, on calculated moves that kept him at the top. And now? Now he was crammed into a worn-down seat, dressed in secondhand clothes Graham had thrown at him before shoving him out the door. A scratchy flannel, a faded T-shirt, and a pair of jeans that didn't quite fit—nothing about this felt real.

A garbled voice crackled over the intercom.

"Next stop, Willow Creek. Passengers departing, please gather your belongings."

Ethan sat up straighter, running a hand over his unshaven jaw. This was it. The last stop before complete obscurity.

The train slowed, the wheels screeching against the tracks. Through the smudged glass of the window, he caught his first glimpse of the town.

Willow Creek.

It looked like something out of a forgotten postcard. A small platform, barely lit by an old lamppost that flickered at the edges. Beyond it, a single street stretched into the heart of town, lined with buildings that looked like they hadn't changed in decades. A diner with a faded sign. A hardware store. A gas station with only one pump. And just beyond, a cluster of houses, their porch lights glowing faintly in the night.

This was the kind of town people passed through, not the kind they stayed in.

Perfect.

The train shuddered to a stop, and Ethan stood, slinging his duffel bag over his shoulder. His legs were stiff from hours of sitting, and for a brief moment, he hesitated.

But then the doors hissed open, and the night air rushed in— cold, sharp, and filled with the scent of rain-soaked pavement.

Ethan stepped out onto the platform.

The moment he did, the train groaned, metal grinding against metal as it lurched forward again. Within seconds, it was gone, swallowed by the darkness, leaving him standing there alone.

For the first time in years, there was no driver waiting for him. No security detail. No assistant holding a schedule.

Just silence.

A neon OPEN sign buzzed weakly in the window of the diner across the street, the only place still awake at this hour. Ethan adjusted the strap of his bag and crossed the empty road, his boots scuffing against the cracked pavement. He pushed open the door, and the bell above jingled softly.

The smell of coffee and frying bacon greeted him, warm and familiar in a way that tugged at something deep in his chest.

The place was almost empty. A lone trucker sat in the corner, hunched over his plate, and behind the counter, a woman stood wiping down the surface with quick, practiced motions.

She looked up at the sound of the bell, her sharp brown eyes locking onto him.

"Kitchen's closing soon," she said, tossing her rag over her shoulder. "You need food or just coffee?"

Her voice was smooth but firm, the kind that didn't tolerate nonsense. She was young—mid to late twenties, with dark auburn hair tied in a loose ponytail, a few strands falling free around her face. Her name tag read Lena.

Ethan hesitated for half a second before sliding onto a stool. "Coffee's fine."

Lena gave him a once-over, her expression unreadable. "Suit yourself."

She grabbed a mug, filled it from the fresh pot behind the counter, and set it in front of him. Ethan wrapped his fingers around the ceramic, the heat grounding him for the first time all night.

Lena leaned against the counter, watching him. "You're new."

Ethan lifted an eyebrow. "That obvious?"

She smirked. "Willow Creek doesn't get a lot of strangers passing through, especially not ones that look like they belong in a city."

Ethan forced a half-smile. "Maybe I just needed a change of scenery."

Lena snorted. "Yeah? Well, hope you like boring. Nothing happens here."

That sounded like exactly what he needed.

Before he could respond, the door swung open again, and a man walked in, his heavy boots thudding against the floor. He was broad-shouldered, dressed in worn-out jeans and a grease-stained work shirt, the kind of guy who spent his days fixing things and didn't have time for nonsense.

"Lena," the man grunted in greeting, nodding toward Ethan with mild curiosity.

"Cal," Lena replied. "You're late."

Cal shrugged, stepping behind the counter and grabbing an apron from a hook. "Boss needed me to fix the fryer before morning."

Lena rolled her eyes but didn't argue. Instead, she turned her gaze back to Ethan. "You got a name?"

A simple question. One he had answered a million times before.

But now, for the first time in his life, he had to lie.

"…Ethan Carter," he said after a beat.

Lena tilted her head slightly, as if testing the weight of his words.

"Well, Ethan Carter," she said, wiping her hands on her apron. "If you're planning to stick around, you'll need more than just coffee. You got a place to stay?"

Ethan hesitated.

Lena caught it.

Her smirk returned. "That's what I thought. Let me guess—no job, either?"

He exhaled, shaking his head. "Not yet."

Cal, who had been tying his apron, snorted. "Good luck. Ain't exactly a booming job market here."

Lena tapped her fingers on the counter, then sighed. "Actually… you any good with tools?"

Ethan frowned. "What?"

"The diner's always got stuff breaking. If you're looking for work, we could use a handyman."

A handyman.

The idea was almost laughable. Ethan Cole had spent his life closing billion-dollar deals, running a corporate empire. And now, he was about to become… a handyman?

But what choice did he have?

He needed to blend in. He needed to disappear.

Ethan met Lena's gaze. "I can handle it."

Lena studied him for another moment before nodding.

"Fine. You start tomorrow."

And just like that, Ethan Cole—the billionaire who once owned the world—became Ethan Carter, the broke handyman in a town where no one knew who he really was.

Three

A Job and a New Life

Ethan woke to the sound of birds. Not the distant, muffled chirping he sometimes heard through his triple-glazed windows back in Manhattan, but the loud, insistent calls of morning birds perched just outside the window of his tiny, unfamiliar room.

The cot beneath him creaked as he shifted, rubbing the sleep from his eyes. The room was barely big enough for the bed and a small dresser shoved against the wall. The air smelled like old wood and faintly of dust, a far cry from the crisp, temperature-controlled atmosphere of his former penthouse.

He sighed.

This was his life now.

After accepting Lena's offer, she had pointed him toward a room for rent above the diner. It was cheap, small, and probably hadn't been updated since the '80s, but it was a roof over his head. And right now, that was enough.

A knock at the door jolted him fully awake.

"Carter! You up?" Lena's voice. Sharp. Impatient.

Ethan groaned and swung his legs over the side of the bed, running a hand over his face. His stubble had grown into something closer to a full beard, and his hair was an unruly mess. He'd have to deal with that later.

He pulled on a clean—relatively speaking—shirt and jeans before yanking open the door. Lena stood on the other side, arms crossed, looking him up and down.

"You look like hell."

Ethan gave her a deadpan look. "Good morning to you too."

Lena smirked but didn't argue. "Your first day starts now. Let's go."

With that, she turned on her heel and headed down the narrow stairs leading to the back entrance of the diner. Ethan followed, stretching out the stiffness in his muscles.

The Job

The diner was already awake, filled with the scent of coffee, sizzling bacon, and something vaguely sweet—pancakes, maybe. A handful of early customers were scattered across the booths, including the trucker from last night and a few older men who looked like they had been coming here for decades.

Lena led him through the kitchen, where a burly man in a grease-stained apron was flipping eggs with the kind of efficiency that came from years of repetition.

"Carter, this is Dwayne," Lena said, nodding toward the cook.

Dwayne grunted without looking up. "Hope you know how to work a wrench."

"We're about to find out," Ethan muttered.

Lena pushed open a back door, revealing the alley behind the diner. A rusted-out generator sat near the entrance, looking dangerously close to death. Beside it, a set of old wooden shelves had collapsed, leaving a pile of junk leaning against the brick wall.

"This is your first job," Lena said, pointing to the generator. "It's been acting up. If you can fix it, I won't have to call in someone who charges more than this place makes in a day."

Ethan crouched beside it, examining the mess of wires and rusted parts. He had no formal experience with this sort of thing, but he wasn't useless. He had spent years overseeing massive projects, hiring engineers, even dabbling in mechanics when he was younger. He had a good eye for how things worked.

Still, it was a far cry from negotiating mergers.

Lena folded her arms. "Well?"

Ethan sighed. "Get me some tools."

Learning the Hard Way

The next hour was a humiliating exercise in trial and error.

It turned out that fixing a generator wasn't as simple as just replacing a part. Every time Ethan thought he had figured something out, something else broke, sending a puff of smoke or a shower of sparks into the air. By the third failed attempt, his hands were covered in grease, and a thin sheen of sweat coated his forehead.

Lena, meanwhile, had made herself comfortable on an overturned crate, watching with an amused smirk.

"Not as easy as you thought, huh, city boy?"

Ethan shot her a glare. "It's Ethan."

She shrugged. "Carter suits you better. Less... polished."

He gritted his teeth and went back to work.

Eventually, after a few more failed attempts and a lot of muttered cursing, the generator rumbled to life. It let out a sputtering cough before settling into a steady hum.

Ethan wiped his hands on his jeans, satisfied.

Lena arched an eyebrow. "Well, I'll be damned. You actually did it."

Ethan smirked. "Doubted me?"

She pushed off the crate and walked past him, her shoulder brushing against his. "Absolutely."

He chuckled, shaking his head.

A Town That Watches

By mid-afternoon, Ethan had tackled two more repair jobs— fixing a leaky sink in the kitchen and patching up a wobbly table in the dining area. He was starting to get the hang of things, though his body was already feeling the strain of manual labor.

As he wiped sweat from his brow, he noticed the old men in the corner booth watching him.

They weren't being subtle about it.

One of them, a wiry guy with a gray beard and an old fishing hat, leaned over to the man beside him and muttered something. The other, a stocky man with weathered hands, just nodded.

Ethan frowned.

Lena must have noticed too, because she leaned against the counter and smirked. "Welcome to Willow Creek. Small town means small-town curiosity."

"They always stare like that?"

"Only when there's something worth staring at." She grabbed a notepad and scribbled something down. "New guy shows up out of nowhere, takes a job as a handyman, but looks like he should be wearing a suit instead? Yeah, you're interesting."

Ethan didn't like the sound of that.

The whole point of coming here was to blend in—not to stand out.

Lena must have seen the flicker of concern in his eyes because she chuckled. "Relax. They'll get used to you. Just don't do anything too weird."

"Define weird."

She smirked. "Anything that makes people start asking real questions."

Ethan nodded slowly, the weight of those words sinking in.

No questions. No attention.

He could do that.

An Unexpected Offer

As the day wound down, Ethan found himself outside again, sitting on the back steps of the diner with a bottle of water. His muscles ached in places he hadn't even known existed.

Lena appeared beside him, holding two beers.

He raised an eyebrow. "Should I be concerned?"

She handed him one. "Consider it your first paycheck."

Ethan took it, twisting off the cap and taking a long sip.

They sat in silence for a moment, the quiet hum of the town settling around them.

Lena glanced at him. "You planning on sticking around?"

Ethan hesitated. He didn't know the answer to that. But for now, he had nowhere else to go.

"I guess that depends," he said.

Lena smirked. "On what?"

Ethan took another sip of his beer and exhaled.

"On whether or not I can actually pull this off."

Lena tilted her head. "Pull what off?"

Ethan met her gaze, something unreadable flickering in his eyes.

"Being someone else."

She studied him for a moment before taking a slow sip of her beer. Then she set the bottle down and stood, stretching.

"Well," she said, heading for the door. "You're off to a damn good start, Carter."

And with that, she disappeared into the diner, leaving him alone with his thoughts.

Ethan leaned back, staring up at the darkening sky.

Maybe, just maybe, he could make this work.

But something told him it wouldn't be that easy.

Four

Clash of Personalities

E than was beginning to learn something about small towns.

They had rules. Unspoken ones, rules that weren't written down anywhere but were understood by every single person who had spent their whole lives there. Rules that an outsider—especially someone like him—wouldn't know until he broke them.

And today, he was about to break a lot of them.

—-

The Morning Rush

The diner was chaos.

Ethan had never seen it this packed before. Every booth was full, the counter lined with customers drinking coffee and flipping through newspapers. The old men from the other day were there, along with a few new faces—people he hadn't seen before but who all seemed to know each other.

Lena was moving between tables like a whirlwind, balancing plates on one arm and refilling coffee cups with the other. Dwayne, the cook, was barking out orders from the kitchen, his face slick with sweat as he flipped pancakes and grilled bacon at an impossible pace.

And Ethan?

Ethan was stuck trying to fix a broken cabinet door in the kitchen while avoiding getting run over.

Lena shot him a glare as she breezed past, barely missing him with a tray of eggs and toast.

"Can you not be in the way?"

Ethan gritted his teeth and tightened the hinge on the cabinet. "I'm fixing it."

"Well, fix it faster."

Before he could respond, she was already out the door, vanishing into the dining area.

Ethan exhaled, rolling his shoulders. He had dealt with difficult people before—CEOs, investors, arrogant board members who thought they knew more than him—but Lena Parker?

She was something else.

And the worst part?

She was right.

He was in the way. He had no idea how to navigate the controlled chaos of this place, and it was pissing him off.

—-

The First Mistake

It started with the coffee machine.

Ethan had noticed it earlier—one of the knobs was loose, the water temperature was inconsistent, and the whole thing looked like it had seen better days. So, while Lena was busy taking orders, he decided to fix it.

Simple enough, right?

Wrong.

Because just as he pulled out his tools, unscrewing the back panel, someone shouted—

"HEY! What the hell is wrong with the coffee?!"

Ethan looked up just in time to see steam pouring from the machine.

Lena appeared in the doorway, eyes wide, murder written all over her face.

"What. Did. You. Do?"

Ethan blinked. "I was fixing it—"

"You were what?!"

Before he could answer, the machine let out a horrible screech, hissed, and then—

BOOM.

A jet of steam shot out the side, sending a hot burst of air through the kitchen. The entire diner went silent. The customers at the counter turned, forks paused halfway to their mouths, staring at the scene like they had just witnessed a crime.

Lena's mouth opened, then closed, then opened again.

Dwayne muttered, "You're a dead man."

Ethan cleared his throat, brushing steam off his arms. "Okay, so that didn't go as planned."

Lena took a slow, deep breath. "Get. Out."

"What?"

She pointed to the back door. "Out. Now."

Ethan hesitated for a second—he was not used to being ordered around like this—but one look at her face and he decided that, for his own safety, it was best to listen.

—-

The Aftermath

Fifteen minutes later, Ethan found himself exiled to the alley behind the diner, sitting on an overturned crate while the cold morning air bit at his skin.

Great.

Just great.

He had been in this town for less than a week, and he had already managed to piss off the one person who had actually given him a job.

The door swung open, and Lena stormed out, slamming it behind her. She folded her arms and glared down at him.

"Let me explain something to you, Carter."

Ethan sighed. "Here we go."

"Rule number one—you don't touch my coffee machine."

He opened his mouth, but she wasn't done.

"Rule number two—you don't fix things that aren't yours to fix. Especially not during the busiest rush of the week."

Ethan rubbed a hand over his face. "I was trying to help."

"Yeah? Well, you almost gave Old Man Jenkins third-degree burns, so maybe don't try so hard."

Ethan frowned. "Who?"

Lena jabbed a finger toward the window. Ethan followed her gaze and spotted an ancient-looking man sitting at the counter, his face still slightly pink from the steam explosion. He was drinking his coffee with shaky hands.

"…That's on me."

"You think?"

Ethan let out a slow breath, forcing himself to stay calm. He had never taken orders from anyone, let alone a feisty waitress with a sharp tongue and an unreasonably good memory. But he wasn't Ethan Cole, billionaire mogul anymore.

He was Ethan Carter, broke handyman.

And if he wanted to stay under the radar, he needed to play the part.

So, instead of snapping back, he looked up at her and said, "Okay. I messed up."

Lena blinked. "What?"

"I messed up," he repeated. "I should have waited. I should have asked. I didn't. Won't happen again."

Lena tilted her head, studying him.

Ethan had the distinct feeling that she wasn't used to people admitting they were wrong.

Finally, she exhaled, rubbing her temples. "God, you're exhausting."

He smirked. "So I've been told."

Lena rolled her eyes but didn't argue. Instead, she pulled a pack of gum from her pocket, popped a piece in her mouth, and then—

"Alright, fine. You're not fired."

Ethan raised an eyebrow. "I was close, though, huh?"

She smirked. "Oh, you have no idea."

For a second, there was something there—something unspoken

in the way she looked at him.

And then, just as quickly, she turned toward the door.

"Come on, Carter. You owe me a new coffee machine."

Ethan groaned, standing up and following her inside.

As he stepped back into the warmth of the diner, he realized something.

This wasn't just about fixing things or earning a paycheck.

This was about earning trust.

And Lena Parker's trust?

That was going to take a hell of a lot more work.

Five

Small Town, Big Secrets

Ethan had always been good at reading people.

It was a skill he had mastered over years of sitting across from board members, investors, and competitors—studying their ticks, their microexpressions, the way they fidgeted when they were lying. It had been the foundation of his success.

And yet, in the past week, he had come to a startling realization.

He couldn't read Lena Parker.

She was unpredictable. Sharp one moment, soft the next. One day, she was shoving a dish rag at him and barking orders; the next, she was handing him a beer at the back steps like they were old friends.

But today?

Today, she was off.

She had been quieter than usual, her usual sarcastic quips toned down, her sharp energy replaced by something more guarded.

Ethan noticed it the moment he stepped into the diner that morning. She was tense—not in an obvious way, but in the way her fingers drummed against the countertop when she thought no one was looking. In the way she glanced at the door every time the bell rang, as if she was expecting someone.

Something was wrong.

And Ethan wanted to know what.

—-

An Uneasy Morning

The diner was slow that day. A few regulars sat in their usual spots, sipping coffee and chatting in hushed tones. The old men in the corner booth kept glancing toward the door, their expressions unreadable.

Ethan grabbed a wrench from the tool kit he kept in the back and made himself busy repairing a loose bolt on one of the kitchen shelves. He worked slowly, keeping an eye on Lena as she moved around the room, taking orders, refilling cups.

She looked distracted. Unsettled.

After a while, she disappeared into the back storage room.

Ethan hesitated for half a second before following.

He found her leaning against a stack of boxes, her arms folded, staring at the wall like she was somewhere else entirely.

"Alright," he said, leaning against the doorframe. "What's going on with you?"

Lena blinked and turned to face him, her expression snapping back into something neutral.

"What are you talking about?"

Ethan gave her a look. "You've been acting weird all morning."

Lena scoffed. "I act weird every morning."

"Not like this."

She rolled her eyes and started moving boxes around, like she was suddenly very interested in organizing supplies that clearly didn't need organizing. "I don't know what you think you're picking up on, but I'm fine."

Ethan crossed his arms. "You keep checking the door. You're waiting for someone."

She stiffened—just slightly, but enough for him to notice.

"Mind your own business, Carter."

Ethan pushed off the doorframe. "Lena—"

The bell above the front door jingled.

Lena froze.

Ethan watched as she inhaled sharply, then exhaled slowly, schooling her features into something unreadable before stepping past him and heading back into the main diner.

Ethan followed.

The moment he stepped out of the back room, he saw who had walked in.

A man stood near the entrance.

Tall. Lean. Mean-looking.

He had the kind of face that made people tense without knowing why—a sharp jaw, sunken cheeks, eyes that didn't blink enough. He wore a denim jacket, his hands stuffed into his pockets, scanning the room with a slow, calculated sweep.

The diner was dead silent.

Even the old men in the corner had stopped talking.

The man's eyes landed on Lena.

And then he smiled.

"Lena." His voice was smooth, too smooth, like oil on water. "Long time no see."

Lena's posture didn't change.

But Ethan, standing just a few feet away, saw the way her fingers curled into fists.

—-

A Man from the Past

Ethan could feel the tension in the air, thick and suffocating.

The way the other customers avoided looking directly at the man told him everything.

This wasn't just some random stranger passing through.

He was someone they knew.

Someone they didn't want here.

Lena stepped forward, arms crossed. "Derek."

Ethan noted the name, filing it away.

Derek tilted his head, his grin widening like he was enjoying some inside joke that no one else was in on.

"You're looking good, Lena."

"Can't say the same for you."

A few of the older men chuckled at that, but no one looked truly amused.

Derek ignored it. He took a step closer, and Ethan saw Lena's jaw tighten.

She didn't move back.

Didn't flinch.

But she was braced.

Ethan had seen that stance before.

Not in boardrooms. Not in business meetings.

In fights.

She was ready for one.

Derek let out a low chuckle. "Still got that sharp tongue, huh?"

Lena's expression didn't waver. "What do you want?"

Derek sighed dramatically, pulling a hand from his pocket and rubbing his chin. "Well, that's a complicated question. See, I was just passing through, and I thought—hey, wouldn't it be nice to check in on an old friend?"

His eyes flickered toward Ethan, assessing him in a way that made his skin crawl.

"And who's this?"

Ethan stayed where he was, meeting Derek's gaze with zero expression.

Lena didn't even look at him.

"None of your damn business."

Derek chuckled. "Fair enough."

Ethan watched, silent but alert, as Derek leaned against the counter like he belonged there.

"You know, Lena, you never were great at making friends," Derek mused. "Always keeping people at arm's length, always acting like you didn't need anyone."

Lena's grip on her own arms tightened.

Derek smiled wider.

"You still owe me."

The words landed like a hammer.

Ethan saw it—the flicker of something in Lena's eyes.

Not fear.

Not panic.

Rage.

"You don't belong here, Derek."

Derek tsked. "That's not very friendly."

"I'm not feeling very friendly."

Silence.

Then—

Derek straightened, adjusting his jacket. "Alright," he said easily. "I'll be seeing you, Lena."

He turned and strolled toward the door, pushing it open and stepping outside without looking back.

The second he was gone, the diner let out a collective breath.

Ethan turned to Lena, studying her.

She was still tense, staring at the door like she was expecting

Derek to walk back in.

Ethan's jaw tightened.

"Lena."

She exhaled, unclenching her hands. Then she turned, her eyes meeting his.

And for the first time since he met her—

She looked away first.

"I don't want to talk about it."

Ethan didn't move.

Didn't push.

But one thing was clear.

Lena Parker had secrets.

And Ethan was going to find out what they were.

Six

A Glimpse of the Past

The diner was unusually quiet that evening, but Ethan knew better than to think things had returned to normal. Nothing about today had been normal.

Lena had barely spoken to him since Derek left. She had gone through the rest of her shift like a woman on autopilot, wiping down tables with a little too much force, refilling coffee cups without actually looking at the people drinking them. She moved like she was somewhere else entirely, locked in thoughts she had no intention of sharing.

Ethan had seen it before.

It was the same way he had moved after his own life had crumbled.

The weight of something unsaid, the exhaustion of carrying a past that refused to stay buried.

And yet, for all the questions spinning in his mind, he didn't push her.

Not yet.

—-

A Silent Ride

By the time the last customer left and Dwayne locked up the kitchen, the night had settled thick and heavy over Willow Creek. Lena tossed her apron on the counter and grabbed her bag without a word.

Ethan hesitated, watching as she made her way toward the door. Then, before he could talk himself out of it, he grabbed his own things and followed her outside.

She didn't react when he fell into step beside her, their footsteps crunching against the gravel of the dimly lit parking lot.

"You always this chatty?" Ethan asked.

Lena didn't slow down. "You don't have to walk me home, Carter."

"Who says I am?"

She shot him a sideways glance. "You don't live this way."

Ethan shrugged. "Maybe I just like long walks."

Lena exhaled sharply, but there was a hint of amusement behind it. She didn't argue, though, which meant she didn't really mind the company.

They walked in silence for a while, past the darkened storefronts and quiet houses, past the old gas station with its single rusted-out pump. There weren't many streetlights in Willow Creek, just the occasional porch light flickering in the distance, casting long shadows across the pavement.

Ethan waited until they were halfway down the road before speaking again.

"You going to tell me who that guy was?"

Lena's footsteps slowed just slightly.

Then—

"Nope."

Ethan smirked. "Didn't think so."

Silence.

Then, after a few more steps—

"He's nobody," Lena muttered.

Ethan arched a brow. "Seemed like somebody."

She sighed. "I don't owe you an explanation."

"You don't," Ethan agreed easily. "But that guy? He wasn't here for a friendly visit."

Lena kept walking, her pace a little quicker now.

"You got a history with him," Ethan continued, watching her carefully. "And judging by the way everyone else reacted when he walked in, it's not a good one."

Lena let out a short laugh, but it lacked any real humor. "You really don't let things go, do you?"

Ethan smirked. "Not in my nature."

They walked another few steps before she finally exhaled, rubbing a hand over her face.

"He used to live here," she said.

Ethan stayed quiet, letting her talk at her own pace.

"He left a few years ago," Lena continued. "Or more like—he ran."

Ethan frowned. "Ran from what?"

Lena shook her head. "Trouble. The kind that doesn't just go away."

Ethan narrowed his eyes, filing that information away. "And now he's back."

Lena's jaw tightened. "Yeah. And that's a problem."

She didn't elaborate, and Ethan didn't press.

But one thing was clear.

Derek wasn't just some guy from Lena's past.

He was a threat.

—-

A Storm Brewing

They reached Lena's house a few minutes later, a small one-story place tucked behind an overgrown fence. The porch light flickered weakly, casting just enough glow to make out the peeling paint on the front steps.

Lena climbed up, unlocking the door, but hesitated before stepping inside.

Ethan leaned against the trailing, crossing his arms.

"You gonna be okay?" he asked.

Lena huffed. "I'm always okay."

Ethan tilted his head, studying her. "Yeah. You keep saying that."

Lena met his gaze, something unreadable flickering in her expression.

Then—just like that—she was closed off again.

"Go home, Carter."

Ethan exhaled through his nose but didn't argue. "See you tomorrow."

Lena didn't respond, just slipped inside and shut the door behind her.

Ethan stood there for a second, staring at the chipped wood of her porch, before finally turning back toward town.

The night was colder now, a sharp wind cutting through the empty streets. He shoved his hands into his pockets and started walking, his thoughts refusing to settle.

Something about this town wasn't right.

And something about Lena's past was even worse.

—-

A Shadow in the Dark

Ethan had just reached his building when he felt it.

That familiar prickle at the back of his neck.

Someone was watching him.

He kept walking, his posture relaxed, his expression unreadable. He had spent too many years around dangerous men to react on instinct alone. If someone was following him, the worst thing he could do was let them know he had noticed.

He turned the corner, stepping into the narrow alley beside the diner. Then, moving quick, he spun around—

And caught a figure in the shadows.

The man froze.

For a split second, they locked eyes.

And then—

He bolted.

Ethan didn't hesitate.

He took off after him, his boots slamming against the pavement, his pulse a steady, focused beat. The man was fast, cutting through the alley with practiced ease, but Ethan was faster.

He caught up just as they reached the end of the alley, grabbing the guy by the back of his jacket and slamming him against the brick wall.

The man grunted, struggling, but Ethan pinned him in place.

"Not a good night for a run," Ethan muttered.

The guy stopped fighting, his breath coming fast. Ethan finally got a good look at him.

Young. Early twenties. Gaunt. Nervous as hell.

And vaguely familiar.

Ethan narrowed his eyes. "I know you."

The guy swallowed hard. "I—I work at the gas station."

Ethan remembered now. He had seen him behind the counter a couple of times. Danny something.

Ethan didn't let go. "Why are you following me?"

Danny hesitated. Then—quietly—

"I wasn't following you," he muttered. "I was watching her."

Ethan's blood ran cold.

Lena.

Ethan's grip tightened. "Why?"

Danny hesitated. Then—

"Because Derek's back."

Ethan's stomach twisted.

Danny's voice was shaky. "You don't know what kind of guy he is. If he's back—it's not for something good."

Ethan already knew that.

But hearing it from someone else?

That made it real.

Ethan released him, stepping back. "Go home, Danny."

Danny hesitated—then took off, vanishing into the night.

Ethan stood there for a long moment, his fists clenching.

Then, slowly, he turned back toward Lena's house.

Because one thing was certain now.

Lena wasn't just dealing with some ex.

She was dealing with something a hell of a lot worse.

Seven

The Past Never Forgets

Ethan didn't sleep much that night.

His mind kept spinning with the same questions, over and over. The image of Lena slamming the door in his face, the shadows in the alley, the way Danny had looked at him—like he knew something Ethan didn't.

He hadn't been in Willow Creek long, but it already felt like he was surrounded by ghosts. The town wasn't just a place—it was a prison built on secrets. And no matter how hard he tried to keep his head down, those secrets were starting to surface.

The thing was, Ethan wasn't used to being in the dark.

For years, he had controlled everything. His company, his image, his entire life. But now? Now, he was just another stranger in a small town with a broken past.

He needed answers.

—-

Morning Shadows

The next day was colder than it had been in a while, a biting wind sweeping through Willow Creek, as if the weather itself was in on the town's unspoken tension. The streets were quieter than usual. The usual hum of daily life—the chatter of town folk, the hum of passing cars—was gone. Today, it felt like the town was holding its breath.

Ethan had woken early, feeling the weight of the night pressing down on his shoulders. He needed to figure out what was really going on with Lena and Derek.

And he had a feeling that today, he was going to find out.

The diner was just as quiet when he arrived, only a few regulars scattered across the counter. Lena wasn't behind the counter yet, so Ethan grabbed a seat near the back, trying his best to blend in. He wasn't expecting anything dramatic, but a part of him hoped something—anything—would give him a glimpse of what Lena was really dealing with.

Lena came in a few minutes later, moving through the kitchen with a forced sense of urgency. She didn't look at him as she passed, didn't even acknowledge his presence. Her movements were stiff, controlled. He could tell something was off, but it was more than just the tension between them from last night—it was deeper than that.

She wasn't acting like herself.

Ethan watched her for a while, waiting for a chance to talk to her.

And then, as if on cue, she glanced over at him. Her eyes flickered for a moment, hesitation crossing her features. Then, she turned and walked straight over to him.

"What do you want, Carter?" Her voice was quiet but firm, and there was a hardness to it that hadn't been there before.

Ethan leaned back in his seat, trying to read her. "I'm not here to cause trouble."

She smirked, but it wasn't a real smile. "No, you're just here to make it worse, huh?"

Ethan shook his head, his gaze steady. "No. I'm here because something's going on with you, Lena. And I want to help."

She flinched at his words, and for the briefest moment, he saw something—vulnerability.

But it was gone as quickly as it had appeared. She folded her arms across her chest, taking a deep breath. "I don't need your help. I don't need anyone's help."

Ethan didn't move. He let the silence stretch between them. There was something in the way she stood, the way she held herself, that made him feel like he was staring into a wall. She was keeping something back, something big.

"I saw him last night," he said quietly, watching her carefully. "Derek. He's not just some guy from your past, is he?"

Her eyes flickered again, this time with a flash of something that looked almost like fear.

"Does it really matter?" she asked.

Ethan didn't answer. He didn't need to.

Lena's gaze dropped to the floor, her lips pressed together tightly. After a long pause, she finally spoke. "You don't know what you're asking, Carter. You don't know who Derek is."

"Then tell me." His voice was low but firm.

She looked up at him, her eyes suddenly sharp. "It's not something I can just explain. It's…" She trailed off, her words heavy with something unspoken.

The tension between them was thick now, the air charged with the weight of the past. And for the first time since he'd arrived in Willow Creek, Ethan had the distinct feeling that he wasn't meant to be here.

But it was too late to back off now.

"I'm not going anywhere," he said quietly.

Lena exhaled sharply, looking at him like she was trying to decide whether to trust him or shove him out the door. Finally, she nodded, but only barely.

"You want to know who Derek is?" She leaned in slightly, her voice dropping to a near-whisper. "He's the reason I left this town."

Ethan's chest tightened. He didn't speak, didn't interrupt. He just listened, waiting for her to continue.

"I was in a bad place when I was younger. A lot of bad things happened, and Derek was at the center of it all. He's the kind of guy who… gets things done. By any means necessary. And he's got a way of making you think you're on his side, even when you're not."

Ethan's brow furrowed. "What kind of things?"

Lena hesitated, her fingers twitching like she was fighting the urge to say more. Finally, she looked up at him, and for the first time, there was a flicker of pain in her eyes.

"You wouldn't understand," she whispered.

Ethan didn't back down. "Try me."

Lena took a long breath, her voice barely audible. "Derek wasn't just a boyfriend. He was the kind of person who could destroy you if you weren't careful. He knew things—about people, about power—and he used that against me. I... I was stupid enough to fall for him."

Ethan's heart dropped into his stomach. He could see the struggle in her, the way her jaw clenched and her eyes flitted nervously around the room. He could feel how much she was holding back, and he understood that this was something she hadn't shared with anyone in a long time—maybe ever.

She took another breath, steadying herself. "I thought I could get away. I thought if I left, I could escape it. But Derek doesn't let people leave. He doesn't let things go."

Ethan stood up slowly, his mind racing. "So now he's back, and you're telling me he's dangerous?"

Lena's eyes flashed with something fierce. "Dangerous isn't even the half of it."

Ethan could feel the weight of her words hanging in the air. This wasn't just about a bad relationship or some difficult breakup. There was more—much more—buried underneath all of this.

"What does he want?" Ethan asked, his voice steady, though his mind was reeling.

Lena hesitated, her eyes darkening. "Power. Control. And he's going to use whatever means necessary to get it."

Ethan's stomach twisted. He didn't know how much longer he could stand the tension in the room, the heaviness of the past creeping into the present. But there was one thing he knew—he wasn't going to let Derek hurt Lena again.

"I won't let him," Ethan said quietly, his eyes meeting hers.

Lena shook her head. "You don't get it. You don't know who you're dealing with."

"I don't care who he is." Ethan's voice was firm, unshakable. "I'm not letting him hurt you."

Lena's eyes softened for a brief moment, but then she shook her head again, backing away.

"You think you can just come in here and fix everything?" Her voice wavered. "You can't. You don't know what Derek's capable of. And you don't know what he's done."

Ethan's chest tightened. "Then tell me."

Lena's gaze dropped, her shoulders slumping in defeat. "I can't."

"Why?"

"Because if I do," she whispered, "it's going to cost me everything."

Ethan stood there, watching her, a cold realization settling deep in his bones.

The past wasn't done with Lena Parker.

And it wasn't done with him either.

56

Eight

Shadows of the Past

The next morning, Ethan felt the weight of the entire town pressing down on him.

Willow Creek had always felt like a place frozen in time—a sleepy, almost idyllic little town where secrets hid behind every corner and nothing ever really changed. But now, it felt like the ground was shifting beneath his feet, as if the entire town was preparing to reveal something dark, something that had been buried for far too long.

Ethan had spent the past few hours pacing in his room above the diner, trying to process everything Lena had said. The tension in the air between them was palpable, and the truth about Derek was something that could no longer be ignored. Ethan had always been someone who prided himself on his control over situations, but now he found himself at the mercy of a small town with a history he didn't understand, and a woman whose pain was too deep for words.

Lena's warning echoed in his mind: You don't know who you're dealing with.

Ethan was beginning to realize that Lena's history with Derek went far deeper than he could have ever imagined. The way she had closed off, the way she had pulled away from him after the briefest moment of vulnerability—it was clear that Derek wasn't just a man from her past. He was a ghost. A figure that loomed over every corner of her life, threatening to pull her back into a darkness she had tried to escape.

Ethan wasn't going to let that happen.

But Lena hadn't made it easy. She had clammed up, retreating into herself, unwilling to give him the full story. That was fine. Ethan didn't need her to open up for him to take action.

The pieces were falling into place.

The door to the diner creaked open just as Ethan was about to leave, and he looked up, expecting to see Lena. But instead, a figure stepped into the room.

It was Danny.

The young man from the gas station. The one who had warned Ethan about Derek the night before.

Danny's eyes darted nervously to the side before he made his way over to Ethan's table. His expression was a mixture of fear and determination, like he wasn't sure whether he was making a huge mistake by coming here or if he was finally doing the right thing.

"You're him, right?" Danny asked, his voice quiet but urgent.

Ethan didn't need to ask who he was talking about. "Yeah. I'm him."

Danny shifted uncomfortably, glancing toward the door as if expecting someone to follow him. The way his hands trembled suggested he was anything but calm.

"Lena... she's in trouble," Danny said, lowering his voice to a near whisper.

Ethan leaned in, his mind immediately snapping into focus. "What kind of trouble?"

Danny hesitated, swallowing hard, before he sat down across from Ethan. His eyes were wide, the fear in them evident.

"It's Derek. He's..." Danny trailed off, looking like he wasn't sure how to continue.

"Spit it out," Ethan urged, his patience growing thin.

Danny looked around once more, then lowered his voice even further. "He's planning something. Something big. I don't know all the details, but I overheard some things, and it's bad. Real bad."

Ethan felt his stomach tighten. "What are you talking about? What's he planning?"

"I don't know," Danny repeated, shaking his head. "But it involves Lena. I know that much. I overheard Derek talking to some guys at the gas station a couple of nights ago. He mentioned getting her back—by force if he had to."

Ethan's blood ran cold. "What does he want with Lena?"

Danny shifted uncomfortably in his seat, his hands clenched into fists. "I don't know. But it's not good. It's never good when Derek's involved. He… he's dangerous, okay? He's been running things in this town for a long time. People might act like nothing's wrong, but they're too scared to speak up. I don't know how much more Lena can take. She's been running from him for years. And now, I think he's finally found a way to drag her back in."

Ethan's mind raced. He hadn't imagined that Derek's return was this calculated, but he should have. Derek had never been the kind of man to let anything slip through his fingers— especially someone like Lena.

"So what do we do?" Ethan asked, his voice steady despite the chaos swirling inside him.

"I don't know, man," Danny said, his voice filled with regret. "I didn't know who else to talk to. I saw the way he looked at you last night. I saw the way he was watching Lena. He's not done. Not by a long shot."

Ethan exhaled slowly, absorbing the information. It was as if everything around him was falling into place, but there were still too many pieces missing. He needed to talk to Lena—he needed to make her understand that this wasn't just some old ghost from her past. Derek had been playing a game, and now, the stakes had been raised.

But Danny's next words stopped him in his tracks.

"I saw him last night, too."

Ethan's head snapped up. "Derek?"

Danny nodded, his voice shaking. "Yeah. He was at the old warehouse on the edge of town. I don't know what he's up to, but something tells me it's got something to do with Lena. I overheard him talking about closing the deal. Whatever it is, it's happening soon."

Ethan's blood turned to ice. The warehouse. It wasn't just some abandoned building—it was a place that had been tied to illegal deals and shady operations for years. No one ever went there unless they were involved in something far worse than they let on.

Ethan stood up quickly, feeling the weight of urgency. "Where is it?"

Danny's hand shot out, grabbing Ethan's wrist. "You can't go there. It's too dangerous. Derek's got people with him—people who don't care about anything except getting the job done. If you go there, you'll be walking right into his trap."

Ethan yanked his wrist free, his jaw tightening. "I don't have time for this. I'm going to find out what's happening."

"Don't say I didn't warn you," Danny muttered, backing away slowly. "Just… don't go near Lena if you can help it. She's already caught up in this mess. You won't be able to pull her out if you get involved."

Ethan ignored him, heading for the door. He didn't need anyone telling him to stay away from Lena. He had to fix this himself, before Derek had the chance to do anything more.

—-

The Warehouse

The drive to the warehouse felt like an eternity. The roads in Willow Creek were quiet, the dark, narrow streets winding through trees and past fields. Every corner he turned, every mile that passed, Ethan could feel the pressure mounting inside him. The warehouse wasn't just some dingy place—it was a place of power, a place where people like Derek didn't just meet; they made deals. And those deals weren't just about money— they were about control. Power. And now, Lena was right in the middle of it.

When Ethan finally reached the edge of town, the air had grown colder, and the sky was beginning to darken. He could see the silhouette of the warehouse in the distance, looming like a ghost over the fields. The building was run-down, its windows boarded up and the paint chipped away by years of neglect. But it was the perfect place for a man like Derek to hide in plain sight.

Ethan parked his truck behind a row of trees, keeping a low profile as he crept closer. He could see movement near the back of the building—shadows shifting against the broken walls.

Ethan's heart raced as he moved silently toward the entrance, his body tense, every sense on high alert. As he drew closer, he could hear voices—muffled but unmistakable. Derek's voice was low, commanding.

And then, another voice—a voice Ethan didn't recognize.

"We're ready. Everything's in place," the man said.

Derek chuckled. "Good. We close this tonight."

Ethan's stomach twisted. It was worse than he'd thought. Derek wasn't just back in town for some unfinished business—he was preparing for something much bigger.

Ethan moved closer, his breath steady, his mind focused on one thing: getting answers.

As he rounded the corner of the warehouse, he froze.

Lena.

She was standing there, just inside the shadows, her face pale, her eyes wide. She was alone.

And Derek wasn't far behind her.

"Lena," Ethan whispered under his breath.

But it was too late. Derek had already seen him.

Nine

The Deal

Ethan's heart skipped a beat as he watched Lena standing just inside the shadows, her body tense, her posture rigid. Derek was so close to her—close enough that Ethan could hear the low murmur of his voice, a sound that carried through the silent night like a snake's hiss. He didn't know how long Lena had been there, but the look on her face—something between defiance and fear—told him she wasn't there willingly.

Everything inside Ethan screamed at him to move, to rush forward and stop whatever was about to happen, but he held himself back. Every muscle in his body was on high alert, his mind racing, trying to process what he was seeing. He had underestimated how deep Derek's roots went in Willow Creek. He had thought Lena could escape him—that she was free. But this moment told a different story. Derek was in control. And

Lena was caught in his web.

Ethan's instincts told him to take action, but he couldn't risk blowing his cover. If Derek knew he was here, the whole plan would be ruined before it even started. He needed to stay calm. He needed to find a way to take control of the situation before things went south. Fast.

—-

The Confrontation

Ethan crept closer, staying low to the ground, using the shadows to hide his movements. The tall, decaying structure of the warehouse loomed over him like a dark sentinel. He couldn't risk moving too fast, but every second that passed felt like an eternity.

He could see Lena now, her face hardening as Derek's voice reached her again, too soft and too menacing to ignore.

"Lena, you know better than this. You know what happens when you try to run from me." Derek's tone was smooth, calculated, the kind of voice that made your skin crawl. Ethan's hands tightened into fists, his jaw set in determination.

Lena didn't respond immediately. She was staring at the ground, her fingers twitching like she was trying to control the trembling in her hands. Ethan could tell she was trying to hold it together, but there was something more—a storm was brewing inside her, something dark and painful, and it was just waiting to break free.

Then, Derek stepped closer to her, his presence a shadow that cast over her small frame. Lena didn't flinch, but Ethan could see her shoulders stiffen.

"I know you're scared, Lena. But it won't matter soon. We'll put all this behind us," Derek said, his voice dripping with false sweetness. He reached a hand out, touching her arm with a soft, almost affectionate gesture.

Ethan's stomach churned. This wasn't just a conversation—it was a manipulation. A power play.

Lena jerked her arm away from Derek's touch. Ethan saw it. It was quick, sharp. But there was something in the way she did it—something that told Ethan she had been practicing this act for a long time. She was playing the game. And for all her bravado, Ethan knew the truth. She was terrified.

"Derek, stop," Lena said, her voice barely above a whisper, but there was an edge to it. Ethan could hear the tremor in her words, and he could feel her pulse, even from this distance. She wasn't as strong as she was trying to appear. She was still too scared. But she was holding on.

Derek's smile faded just a fraction. "What did you say?"

Lena straightened, her jaw set. "I'm not going back to you, Derek. I'm done."

For the first time since he had laid eyes on her, Ethan saw a flicker of something real in Lena's eyes. Fear. Defiance. It was a dangerous combination.

Derek's eyes darkened. "You think you have a choice? You think you can just walk away from me? I own this town, Lena. I own you. You can't escape me."

Ethan took a deep breath, watching them, waiting for the right moment. He could feel his heart pounding in his chest. No more games. He couldn't just watch this happen. He had to act.

He took a step forward, his boots crunching against the gravel beneath him, but the sound was enough to draw Derek's attention.

—-

The Showdown

Derek turned, his eyes narrowing. The moment he saw Ethan, his lips curled into a smile—a predator spotting fresh prey. "Well, well. Looks like the little city boy has come to play."

Ethan didn't flinch, though his fists were clenched so tight that his knuckles ached. He took a slow, deliberate step forward, his eyes locked on Derek.

"I'm not here for games, Derek. I'm here for Lena," Ethan said, his voice steady and unyielding.

Derek chuckled darkly, the sound echoing in the vast emptiness of the warehouse. "You think you can stop me? You think she's going to let you get in the way of this?"

Lena was silent now, her gaze shifting between the two men, her body stiff, almost as if she didn't know what to do next. She was caught between two forces, both of them vying for control, for something Lena had kept buried inside her for years.

"You're making a mistake, Derek," Ethan said, his voice low, but it carried the weight of everything he had learned about the man. He wasn't just a criminal—he was a manipulator. He thrived on control, on keeping people like Lena under his thumb. And Ethan wasn't going to let that happen.

Derek's eyes flicked between him and Lena, sizing up the situation. "A mistake? No, I think you're the one making a mistake." His voice dropped, his smile widening with menace. "You don't know anything about her, do you? You don't know how far she'll go to protect her little secrets."

Ethan could feel the tension rising, the air thick with unspoken threats. "She's not yours to control, Derek."

Derek's expression darkened, his face contorting with rage. "You're not the first person to think they can take something from me, but you'll be the first to regret it."

For a brief moment, Derek's hand moved to his coat pocket, and Ethan's instincts screamed at him to act. But before he could move, Lena's voice rang out, sharp and cutting through the air.

"No, Derek. Don't."

Both men turned toward her in surprise. She was standing taller now, her shoulders squared, her voice more resolute. "This is over. I won't let you destroy everything just to get your way. I'm done."

Ethan's heart skipped. He knew what was coming next. This was her moment. She wasn't just fighting for herself anymore. She was fighting for something much bigger than that. But she wasn't alone anymore.

Ethan took another step forward, his gaze steady and unblinking. "It's over, Derek. For you."

Derek's eyes flashed with anger, and in that instant, everything seemed to freeze. Ethan felt it, the tension thick and ready to explode. The words they had exchanged, the power play that had been building—this was the moment it all came to a head.

Without warning, Derek pulled a gun from his jacket, aiming it directly at Ethan. His hand was steady, but his eyes were wild with something that could only be described as insanity.

Ethan's breath caught, his body instinctively going into fight-or-flight mode. But before he could react, Lena stepped between them, her arms outstretched, her body blocking the barrel of the gun.

"Don't you dare," she said, her voice shaking but filled with something that could only be described as resolve.

Derek stopped, his hand tightening around the gun. "Lena…" His voice was low, the threat hanging in the air like a suffocating cloud.

"You'll kill me before you ever get what you want," she said, her eyes locked on him, unyielding.

For a moment, time seemed to stand still. Derek's eyes flickered, uncertainty creeping into his gaze as he looked at the woman who had once been under his control—and now, stood in defiance.

And in that brief moment of hesitation, Ethan made his move.

He lunged, grabbing Derek's arm and forcing it down, knocking the gun to the ground. Derek fought back, his strength matching Ethan's, but he wasn't prepared for the fury in Ethan's eyes. Ethan didn't think. He just acted.

The two men struggled on the ground, rolling in the dirt and gravel. But Ethan was stronger. He had no intention of losing. Derek, on the other hand, was desperate. As they grappled, Derek's hand shot out, aiming for Ethan's throat, but Ethan was faster.

In a flash, he was on top of Derek, pinning him down, his forearm pressed against the man's neck. Derek's breath came in ragged gasps, his eyes wide with panic as he realized he had lost control.

Lena stood behind them, breathless, watching as Ethan finally disarmed Derek. She had taken the first step toward freedom, but she wasn't alone anymore. Neither of them was.

Ten

Breaking Point

The fight between Ethan and Derek felt like it lasted an eternity, though in reality it was only a matter of minutes. The warehouse, once an echo of abandonment, now rang with the sound of heavy breathing and grunting, the low growl of desperation in Derek's voice.

Ethan's hands were locked around his adversary's wrist, forcing the gun out of Derek's grip. The man beneath him fought like a cornered animal, thrashing and swearing, but Ethan's hold was unrelenting.

Derek's body stiffened as he struggled to free himself, his eyes wide with rage. "You think you can stop me? You think she is worth this?" he snarled. His teeth were bared, his expression twisted with fury and something darker—fear.

Ethan didn't speak. He didn't need to. Words weren't going to stop this. Only action would.

With a final wrench, he knocked Derek's arm to the side, his grip tightening like steel. The gun skittered across the ground, out of reach. Ethan's chest heaved with adrenaline, and for the first time since the fight began, he realized just how close to losing control he'd come.

Derek's face turned purple, the struggle in his eyes becoming less about strength and more about survival. His breathing was labored, his body wracked with tremors. He tried to move, to throw Ethan off, but Ethan had him pinned.

"You're done, Derek," Ethan said, his voice quiet but firm, each word dropping like a hammer.

Derek's eyes burned with hatred. "You think you've won?" he spat. "This is my town. This is my world, Cole. You don't know who you're dealing with."

The venom in his words only made Ethan tighten his grip. "I think I'm learning," he said coldly. "And I'm done being your pawn."

Lena's voice interrupted the silence that followed. "Ethan, stop."

Ethan's heart skipped a beat as he turned to look at her. She stood just a few feet away, her body rigid, her eyes wide with a combination of fear and something else—something softer, something vulnerable.

She was shaking, her arms folded tightly over her chest, but her stance was solid, like she had made a decision. A decision that had led her here. To this moment.

Ethan slowly loosened his hold on Derek, but he didn't let go entirely. He didn't trust the man lying beneath him, gasping for air, his face contorted in pain. But he also didn't want to give Lena the wrong impression. He didn't want to escalate this. He had already done enough.

Derek's breathing slowed, but the look he gave Lena was venomous. "You don't know what he's doing, do you? You think you're saving him, but all you're doing is helping him make your mistakes for you."

Lena's eyes flickered, a flash of anger passing through her before she took a step toward Ethan. "I'm done listening to you," she said, her voice tight with conviction.

Ethan released Derek completely, pushing himself off the ground. He stepped back, his gaze never leaving the man lying there, his chest heaving as he struggled to regain control.

"You don't get to talk to her like that," Ethan said, his voice low, full of a quiet but seething fury.

Derek shifted, glaring at both of them. "You think she's some kind of prize?" he sneered. "You think you can just waltz into my life, into this town, and fix things? You don't belong here."

Ethan stepped forward, his body tense with the need to end this, but Lena put a hand on his arm, stopping him.

"No," she said, her voice calm but unwavering. "Let him talk. Let him prove he hasn't changed."

Ethan looked at her, the confusion in his eyes matching the flicker of uncertainty that crossed her face. What was she doing? But he didn't question her. Not now. He couldn't.

Lena turned to Derek, her face hardening. "You're right about one thing, Derek. I don't belong here. I never did. But I'm not going back to you. Not ever."

Derek's lips curled into a twisted smile. "You think I'm going to let you walk away again, Lena? After everything we've been through?"

"Everything you put me through," Lena corrected, her voice steady, but the depth of pain in her words was unmistakable. "I'm done, Derek. I'm not your possession anymore. I'm not anyone's."

Derek's eyes darkened, his gaze shifting from Lena to Ethan and back again. "This isn't over," he spat. "You'll both regret this. You can't just erase me. I'll be back. I always come back."

Ethan's heart pounded in his chest, the weight of Derek's threat lingering in the air like smoke. But Lena didn't flinch. She held her ground, standing tall, her shoulders squared.

"I don't care," she said firmly. "Go. Leave this town and never come back. Or I swear, I'll make sure everyone knows what you really are."

Derek stared at her for a long moment, his jaw clenched tight, his eyes narrowing in pure hatred. And then, without another word, he pushed himself to his feet, his movements jerky and disoriented. He staggered back, glancing at Ethan one last time, his lips twisting into a bitter sneer.

"You haven't seen the last of me," Derek said quietly, before turning and disappearing into the darkness, his figure swallowed by the shadows.

The silence that followed felt like a punch to the gut. Ethan stood still, watching as Derek vanished, the night swallowing him whole. But something was different now. Lena had taken a stand. She had broken free, not just from Derek, but from the fear that had held her in his grip for years.

Ethan turned to her, his heart still racing, but his focus entirely on her. She was breathing hard, her body tense with the aftermath of what had just happened.

Lena shook her head slowly, almost as if trying to shake off the remnants of Derek's presence. "I can't believe it's finally over. I can't believe he's gone."

Ethan stepped closer, carefully, cautiously. "It's not over, Lena. He's not gone. Not yet."

She didn't respond at first, her eyes downcast, her face unreadable. Then, she looked up at him, her gaze soft but filled with a kind of sorrow that made his chest tighten.

"I don't know how to let go of it, Ethan," she whispered. "All these years, I've been running from him. And now… I'm not sure how to stop running from the ghost he left behind."

Ethan's heart hurt as he reached out, placing a hand gently on her arm. He could see the pain in her eyes—the same pain he had once carried. The fear that came with realizing you couldn't outrun your past forever.

"You don't have to do it alone," he said softly, his voice steady despite the storm brewing inside him.

Lena swallowed hard, her breath shaky. "I don't know if I can trust anyone again, Ethan. I don't know if I can—"

"You don't have to trust anyone right now," he interrupted gently. "But you don't have to carry this burden by yourself either. We'll figure this out. Together."

She looked at him for a long moment, her eyes searching his face as if looking for something—something to hold onto. Slowly, she nodded, but there was something hesitant in her movements, something she wasn't saying.

Ethan didn't push her. He didn't need to. He knew that right now, the most important thing was that they had survived this together. And together, they would face whatever came next.

—-

The night stretched on, still and heavy, but the air felt a little bit lighter. The battle had been fought. The deal had been broken. And Derek, for now, had been defeated.

But Ethan knew better than to think it was truly over.

In this town, where secrets never stayed buried for long, the true fight had just begun.

Eleven

The Calm Before the Storm

The morning after the confrontation with Derek, the world felt still, like the calm that follows a thunderstorm. The tension in Willow Creek was palpable, thick in the air like smoke lingering after a fire. The town was holding its breath, waiting for the storm to break.

Ethan couldn't shake the feeling that the worst was yet to come.

He hadn't slept much the night before. Every time he closed his eyes, he saw Lena's face—eyes wide, the tension in her body as Derek's anger boiled over. He saw the way Lena had stood up to Derek, not backing down, not retreating even though every part of her must've wanted to. She was strong, but Ethan could feel the toll it had taken on her.

But they weren't done yet.

Derek might have retreated for now, but Ethan knew this wasn't over. The way Derek had spoken, the venom in his voice—it made it clear that this was just the beginning of something far darker.

Ethan knew what he had to do next. He needed to make sure that Derek would never come back, that the man couldn't hurt Lena—or anyone—again. He needed to end this, once and for all.

—-

An Unexpected Visitor

It was a little after noon when the knock came on the door.

Ethan was sitting at the kitchen table, going over the plans he had started to form. He'd gone to the local police station early that morning, only to find the same apathy that had pervaded Willow Creek for years. The sheriff had known Derek's name, had known his history in the town, but was unwilling to lift a finger to stop him. There was no interest in dealing with someone like Derek—no one wanted to make waves in a small town where everyone kept to their own business.

It made Ethan sick. But it also gave him no choice. He would have to take care of it himself.

The knock at the door interrupted his thoughts.

He frowned. He wasn't expecting anyone.

When he opened it, standing in the doorway was Lena.

Her face was pale, her eyes red-rimmed, and there was something in the way she held herself—a weight, like she had been carrying something heavy for far too long.

Ethan stepped aside wordlessly, letting her in.

Lena didn't speak right away. She just walked into the small room, looking like a woman who had just woken up from a nightmare she couldn't quite shake.

Ethan closed the door behind her, his heart in his throat. He had no idea what was going through her head, but the look in her eyes told him it wasn't good.

"Lena, what's wrong?" he asked quietly.

She exhaled shakily, finally looking up at him. "You were right, Ethan," she said, her voice tight with emotion. "This isn't over."

Ethan's stomach twisted. "What happened?"

She bit her lip, a tear escaping before she wiped it away quickly. "I saw him again. Last night."

Ethan's heart skipped a beat. "Derek?"

Lena nodded. "He came by the diner—just after closing. I didn't know what to do. He was… he was calm. Too calm. He said he wanted to talk. Said we needed to finish what we started."

Ethan felt a cold shiver creep down his spine. "What did he want?"

Lena shook her head. "I didn't let him talk for long. I couldn't. But it was clear—he didn't come to make peace. He's planning something, Ethan. Something bad. I don't know exactly what it is, but he's been talking to people in town—getting people on his side."

Ethan's mind raced. "Who?"

Lena stepped closer, lowering her voice. "I don't know. But he mentioned something about backing up a deal. He said the town was going to have to make a choice."

Ethan's jaw clenched. "What kind of deal?"

She shrugged, but the fear in her eyes was unmistakable. "I don't know, Ethan. But I don't think it's just about me anymore. Derek's trying to drag everyone into this—trying to make them choose a side."

Ethan exhaled slowly, his thoughts tumbling over one another. This wasn't just about Derek and Lena anymore. This was about control—about power—and Willow Creek was caught in the middle.

He knew he had to act. But he wasn't sure how to stop something that had already gained so much momentum.

—-

The Choice

The rest of the afternoon passed in a blur. Ethan and Lena sat together at the kitchen table, each of them lost in their own thoughts, trying to piece together a plan. Every moment that passed felt like the calm before a storm, a storm that neither of them could avoid anymore.

Lena had gone quiet after her initial revelation, her hands shaking as she picked at the edge of the table. Ethan could see how much this was eating at her. She had already fought so hard to escape Derek's grasp, but now it felt like she was being dragged back into it.

Ethan didn't know how to make things right. But he had to try.

Finally, after what felt like an eternity, Lena spoke again. Her voice was soft, but there was something in it that made Ethan's blood run cold.

"He's not just going to let me go," she said. "He wants me back. But it's more than that. I heard him talking about a deal with the mayor. I don't know what it is, but I think it's something that could change this whole town."

Ethan sat up straighter. "The mayor?"

Lena nodded. "Yeah. And the sheriff too. Derek's been playing people for years, Ethan. He has connections. He knows how to manipulate people—how to get what he wants. And he's doing it all over again."

Ethan's mind raced. He knew that Derek was dangerous, but this… This was something else entirely. Derek wasn't just running a small-time scheme—he was infiltrating the town, using its people to get what he wanted. And no one, not even the authorities, had the courage to stand up to him.

Ethan clenched his fists. "We need to go to the police. The real police. We need to take this to someone who can stop him."

Lena shook her head, her eyes filled with regret. "It won't work. Not here. I've tried before. Derek's got too many people in his pocket. The mayor, the sheriff—they won't help us. They're in on it."

Ethan froze. "What do you mean they're in on it?"

Lena hesitated, looking down at her hands. "I overheard a conversation. A couple of weeks ago, I heard Derek talking about some deal—something that would make him untouchable. He's been working with the mayor and the sheriff to cover up his operations. They've been helping him keep people like me quiet. The people in this town… they're either too scared to speak up or they're getting something out of it."

Ethan's heart pounded. This was bigger than he thought. This wasn't just about Derek. This was about a whole system—one that had been compromised.

"What do we do?" he asked, his voice low.

Lena looked up at him, her eyes full of something he couldn't quite name. "We have to make a choice, Ethan. We can keep fighting, but it's going to be a battle. And if we lose… if we fail… Derek wins. He takes over."

Ethan nodded slowly. He could feel the weight of her words pressing down on him. This wasn't a fight they could win on their own. They needed help. They needed to expose Derek for who he was. But how?

—-

The Plan

By the time night had fallen, the two of them had come up with a plan. It wasn't perfect. In fact, it was far from it. But it was all they had.

Ethan's mind was still racing, but he knew one thing: They had to break Derek's hold on Willow Creek. If they didn't, the town would belong to him, and nothing would ever change.

Lena had agreed to confront the mayor, but only if they could find a way to prove Derek's involvement. They had to gather enough evidence to force his hand—something the authorities couldn't ignore. It was a long shot, but it was the only chance they had left.

And they had to move fast. Derek wasn't going to wait around. He had already made it clear that he wasn't done. The time to act was now.

As Lena prepared to leave, Ethan turned to her, his voice low. "Whatever happens, I'll be there. We'll face this together."

She nodded, her gaze steady, but there was a sadness in her eyes. "Thank you, Ethan. For everything."

And just like that, the door closed behind her, leaving Ethan standing in the empty room, his mind racing with the reality of what was to come. The storm was coming—and it was up to him and Lena to face it head-on.

Twelve

The Gathering Storm

The streets of Willow Creek were eerily quiet that night, as if the town itself was holding its breath, waiting for the inevitable. The hum of the usual small-town noises—the chatter from the diner, the idle conversations at the corner store, the sounds of dogs barking in the distance— had all faded into an unsettling silence. The air was thick with anticipation, tension hanging like an unspoken promise.

Ethan paced in his small apartment, eyes flicking to the clock every few seconds. Time felt like it was both moving too fast and too slow at the same time. Lena had left hours ago to meet with the mayor, and though he knew she was strong, he couldn't shake the gnawing feeling in the pit of his stomach. Everything was on the line now—everything.

If they didn't expose Derek tonight, if they didn't prove he was trying to take control of the town, then all their efforts would have been for nothing. And if they failed…

Ethan's mind flashed back to the encounter at the warehouse. Derek's venomous words, his threats, his twisted smile that made Ethan's blood run cold. He knew Derek would stop at nothing to get what he wanted. And Lena? She was more than just an obstacle to him. She was his past, his greatest asset, and the one person Derek couldn't seem to control anymore.

Ethan's hands clenched into fists. He wouldn't let Derek win. He couldn't. Not now, not after everything they had gone through.

The sound of a car engine cut through the silence, and Ethan rushed to the window, peering out at the street. His breath caught when he saw the black sedan pulling up in front of the mayor's office. It was sleek, the kind of car that screamed power, that reeked of corruption and dirty deals. Derek's car.

Ethan's heart began to race. This was it. This was the moment.

He grabbed his jacket and slipped out the back door of the building, moving quickly through the alley to stay out of sight. He had no idea what kind of deal was going down inside the mayor's office, but he wasn't about to sit by and wait for things to unfold. Not now. Not when Lena was involved.

—-

The Mayor's Office

Lena had barely made it inside the mayor's office before the door clicked shut behind her. The atmosphere was cold, tense, as though the walls themselves were conspiring to keep the truth hidden.

The mayor, a heavyset man in his late fifties, sat behind his cluttered desk, his fingers tapping nervously on a file. His gray hair was thinning, his tie slightly crooked, but it was the eyes that gave him away. The eyes that betrayed the man who had built his career by making deals with people like Derek. The man who had turned a blind eye to the ugliness lurking beneath the town's surface.

Lena didn't sit. She couldn't. The last time she had been here, she had trusted the mayor. The last time, she had hoped that someone—anyone—would help her escape Derek's clutches. But she'd learned the hard way that the world wasn't made for people like her. The world wasn't made for people who tried to escape their past.

"Lena," Mayor Whitfield said, his voice smooth, too smooth. "I didn't expect to see you back here so soon."

Lena forced a smile, though it felt more like a grimace. "I didn't expect to be here either."

"Is that so?" He raised an eyebrow, a smirk playing at the corners of his lips. "What can I do for you? I thought you were done with us. Done with Willow Creek."

Lena's stomach twisted, but she held her ground. She wouldn't back down. Not this time. "I'm not here for you, Whitfield. I'm here for Derek."

At the mention of Derek's name, the smile faltered. The mayor's eyes shifted, a hint of unease creeping into his expression. But only for a moment. He quickly masked it, his tone becoming more guarded. "What about him?"

"I know what's been going on," Lena said, her voice steady but filled with a quiet intensity. "I know about the deal you made with him. About the control he's trying to gain over this town. And I'm not going to let it happen."

The mayor's fingers stopped tapping the file. He leaned back in his chair, his eyes narrowing. "Lena, you're not in a position to make threats. You know how this works. Derek and I have an understanding. He's a man of power. You don't bite the hand that feeds you."

Lena felt a flicker of disgust rise in her chest. She had tried to run from this, tried to distance herself from the corruption, but it was everywhere. Even in the people who should have been there to protect her. The ones who had turned their backs on her and every other person who had ever been trapped under Derek's thumb.

"You're wrong," she said, her voice low but filled with defiance. "This isn't about power anymore. It's about control. It's about a town that's been ruled by fear for far too long."

The mayor chuckled darkly, a hollow sound that bounced off

the walls. "Fear is what keeps the peace, Lena. Without it, everything would fall apart. You've always known that."

Lena clenched her fists at her sides. "I'm done living in fear."

Before the mayor could respond, there was a knock at the door. Both of them froze, the tension in the room rising immediately. The mayor's face tightened, and without waiting for a response, he stood and walked to the door.

Lena stood still, her breath shallow, her heart pounding. Something about the way the mayor had reacted to the knock— his hurried movement—made her uneasy.

When the door opened, she saw a figure in the doorway. It was Derek.

Her heart dropped into her stomach as his cold, calculating eyes met hers. His face was expressionless, but his presence in the room sent a chill through the air. Derek's voice was like silk, smooth and dangerous.

"Well, well, well. What do we have here?" he said, his eyes flicking between Lena and the mayor. His smile was predatory, and for the first time, Lena realized the full extent of his power. He wasn't just a man with a reputation—he was a man who owned the people around him.

"Derek," Lena whispered, her voice trembling slightly.

"I hope I'm not interrupting," he said, his eyes gleaming with amusement. He stepped into the room, his gaze never leaving Lena's. He could sense her fear, the way she shifted under his scrutiny, but he also knew she was different now. She wasn't the same girl who had once cowered in his shadow.

Derek turned to the mayor, his tone changing to something far colder. "Whitfield, I trust our business is going smoothly?"

The mayor swallowed, his hands wringing in front of him. "Yes, of course. Everything is as planned."

Ethan's voice suddenly cut through the tension. "No. It's not."

The door behind Derek slammed open, and Ethan stepped inside, his presence like a shockwave that rattled the room. He was calm, but there was something dangerous in his eyes as he locked onto Derek.

The mayor's face turned pale as he looked between the two men. "What is this?" he demanded, his voice cracking.

Lena's heart raced, a surge of relief flooding her veins at the sight of Ethan, but she knew they were still far from safe.

Ethan's gaze never left Derek. "This ends tonight."

Derek's smile faltered just slightly, but he didn't back down. "You've made a mistake, Ethan," he said, his voice low and menacing. "You should have stayed out of this."

"Not a chance," Ethan replied coldly. "You're done."

Lena watched as the two men squared off, the tension between them thick and suffocating. She could feel it, the clash of wills, the impending explosion of violence. But this time, it wasn't just about Derek. It was about everything he had tried to destroy—everything he had taken from her, from all of them.

And she wouldn't let him win.

The room was silent for a beat, each of them waiting for the other to make the first move. Then, in a flash, everything changed. Derek's hand shot out toward his jacket, but before he could reach for whatever weapon he had hidden there, Ethan moved.

The air was thick with the sound of the struggle as Derek and Ethan collided, each of them fighting for control, for dominance. The mayor stood frozen, his face pale with fear, unable to do anything but watch as the two men fought for control of the room.

Lena stepped forward, her heart pounding in her chest. She couldn't just stand by. Not this time.

This was the moment. This was her chance to break free from the chains that had held her for so long.

And she wasn't going to waste it.

Thirteen

Unraveling the Lies

The warehouse loomed in the distance, its silhouette stark against the dying light of dusk. A thick fog had begun to roll in from the river, clinging to the edges of the street and twisting through the broken windows of abandoned buildings. Willow Creek was a town of secrets, and tonight, Ethan felt like the air itself was heavy with them.

His mind was still racing from the confrontation with Derek and the mayor. The weight of everything that had just happened—the threats, the lies, the power games—had left him reeling. They were closer than ever to exposing Derek for the manipulative monster he truly was, but something was missing. There were pieces of the puzzle he couldn't see, threads that hadn't been pulled yet, and the closer they got to the truth, the more dangerous it became.

The soft scrape of gravel beneath his boots was the only sound in the otherwise silent night as he approached the warehouse. He could feel the weight of Lena's earlier words echoing in his mind. She had said that Derek's plans were bigger than just a few shady deals. That Derek's ambitions reached deeper into the town than anyone realized. Ethan had come to understand what that meant over the past few days. It wasn't just about taking control of Willow Creek—it was about control everywhere. Derek wanted power, and he would stop at nothing to get it.

As Ethan approached the doors of the warehouse, he scanned the area, his senses on high alert. Everything was quiet, but the quiet made him nervous. He'd learned that the most dangerous moments often arrived in the stillness. He pulled the collar of his jacket up around his neck, taking a deep breath before stepping forward, each movement calculated, deliberate.

The air in the warehouse was thick with dust. The dim light from a single, flickering bulb cast shadows across piles of crates and metal beams. The whole place smelled of decay—of years of abandonment. But there was something else in the air, a sense of urgency, a feeling that whatever was about to happen would change everything.

Ethan's hand tightened around the gun at his side. He wasn't sure what he was walking into, but he knew one thing: he had to be ready.

He crept inside, careful not to make a sound, his boots light on the cracked concrete. He passed rows of crates, each one stacked haphazardly, like they had been thrown into the building in a hurry.

As he rounded the corner, he froze.

In the center of the warehouse stood Derek, his back to Ethan, his arms crossed over his chest. The shadows cast by the dim light made him look even more imposing, his figure exaggerated, like a predator waiting to strike.

"Did you really think you could stop me?" Derek's voice echoed through the empty space, low and mocking. He didn't turn around, didn't even flinch when Ethan's presence became known. He was still in control.

Ethan took a slow step forward, his voice calm but filled with anger. "I'm done watching you destroy this town, Derek. This is the last time you'll threaten anyone."

Derek's laughter bounced off the walls of the warehouse, the sound chilling. "You're naïve, Ethan. You think you can stop me? You think you can just waltz in here and undo everything I've worked for?"

Ethan narrowed his eyes, stepping closer, his mind sharp and focused. "I'm not the one who's destroying lives here. You're the one who's been pulling strings, manipulating people for years. It ends tonight."

Derek slowly turned around, a smirk curling on his lips. "You think you can just walk in here and talk to me like that? You have no idea who you're dealing with."

Ethan clenched his jaw, but he didn't react. He couldn't afford to let his emotions get the best of him—not now, not when everything was so close to unraveling.

Derek's eyes flicked to the side, his gaze lingering on something Ethan couldn't see. Then he turned back, his smirk widening into something darker.

"I'm not the one who's in control anymore," Derek said, his voice laced with amusement. "It's all out in the open now. The deal is sealed."

Ethan's heart skipped a beat. "What deal?"

Derek took a step closer, his hands still folded across his chest. "I've been orchestrating this for a long time, Ethan. I had to play the long game. The mayor, the sheriff, half the town's leaders—they're all in on it. I've been pulling the strings behind the scenes. And you? You think you're the hero? You're nothing but a pawn in this game."

Ethan's stomach tightened. This was worse than he had imagined. Derek hadn't just been after Lena—he had been after everything. The power, the control, the manipulation of the town's very foundation. He had infiltrated every level, every authority. Everyone in his pocket, everyone too scared to stand against him.

Ethan forced himself to stay calm, to think. He wasn't going to let Derek win. Not after everything they had fought for.

"And Lena?" Ethan asked, his voice tight. "What part does she play in all this?"

Derek's smirk faltered for a brief moment, then returned in full force. "Lena? She's the catalyst. The one thing I've always wanted, and she's too blind to see it. She's been running from me for years, but she can't hide forever. She'll come back to me. They all do."

Ethan's hands clenched into fists, his knuckles white with the pressure. "Not this time," he said, his voice barely above a whisper, but filled with a conviction he hadn't had before.

Derek's eyes glinted with something dark, something predatory. "You think you can stop me? I have the town behind me. You don't even know the half of it. This place, this whole place is mine."

Ethan felt the cold edge of a plan forming in his mind, but it was risky. It was dangerous. If it went wrong, everything would fall apart. But there was no other choice. He had to stop Derek.

He took a deep breath and spoke, his voice low. "I won't let you hurt anyone else."

Derek's laugh was cold, and he took a step forward, closing the gap between them. "You think you have control here? You have no idea what you're up against. If you're so desperate to save this town, then I'll show you just how far this will go."

Before Ethan could react, Derek's hand shot out, pulling something from his jacket pocket. It was a small device, a detonator.

Ethan's blood ran cold as Derek's eyes gleamed with a mad excitement. "This warehouse? It's not just a storage room. It's my backup plan. You've been so busy trying to stop me, but you missed the real game. You missed the truth."

The cold, horrifying reality hit Ethan in waves. The warehouse wasn't just a hideout—it was a bomb. Derek had rigged it to explode. He wasn't planning to just walk away from this. He was planning to blow everything up.

"You wouldn't…" Ethan's voice faltered as he processed the implications of Derek's words.

Derek's smile widened. "Wouldn't I? You see, Ethan, I have everything in place. I've been planning this for so long, and now? Now I just get to sit back and watch as it all comes crashing down."

Ethan's mind raced. He had to stop this—now. He couldn't let Derek's plans succeed. He couldn't let him destroy everything Lena had fought for, everything this town had worked to build.

The time for talking was over.

Ethan lunged forward, knocking the detonator from Derek's hand. They collided in a blur of motion, fists flying, adrenaline surging. Derek wasn't the type to give up easily. His strength matched Ethan's, his desperation only fueling the violence between them. But Ethan was focused—he had to be. He couldn't afford to be distracted. The entire warehouse was a ticking time bomb, and he needed to stop it.

With a final, forceful push, Ethan shoved Derek against a stack of crates, sending him crashing to the ground. He rushed to the detonator, quickly pressing the button to disarm it. The seconds seemed to stretch out forever as he fumbled with the device. One wrong move, and everything would be over.

Finally, the screen on the detonator went dark. The threat was neutralized.

Ethan exhaled slowly, his hands still trembling from the adrenaline. He looked over at Derek, who was now lying on the ground, panting heavily. His face was flushed with anger, but there was something else in his eyes—fear.

"You're finished," Ethan said, his voice cold.

Derek didn't respond. He was too stunned, too defeated. And for the first time, Ethan realized that this—this was the moment they had won.

But it wasn't over. Not yet.

Ethan turned to the door, his heart still racing, as the first sound of sirens could be heard in the distance. This was just the beginning.

The storm had come—and now, it was time to rebuild.

Fourteen

The Reckoning

The sirens were louder now, growing steadily closer. Ethan stood frozen in the middle of the warehouse, the dim light flickering above his head as his heart pounded in his chest. The detonator had been disarmed, but the rush of adrenaline that had fueled him only minutes before was beginning to dissipate, leaving behind a knot of unease.

Derek was still on the floor, gasping for breath, his face twisted with fury and disbelief. Ethan watched him carefully, ready to act at the slightest provocation. For all the bravado Derek had shown earlier, there was something different now. The man was broken—not physically, but mentally, emotionally. It was as though the last thread of his control had snapped.

And Lena? Lena was safe. That was the only thing that mattered now.

The sound of the approaching police cars, the flash of blue and red lights spilling through the broken windows of the warehouse, made Ethan tense. He needed to get out before the authorities arrived.

But his gaze never left Derek, who was slowly starting to rise to his feet, his hands pressed against the cold concrete to push himself up. There was something almost pitiful in the way Derek moved now—no longer the confident, calculating figure he had been when he'd walked into the warehouse. Instead, he was a man on the edge, desperate to hold onto whatever shred of power he had left.

Ethan took a step forward, his voice low but firm. "This is it, Derek. No more games."

Derek's head snapped up, his eyes flashing with something dark—something that wasn't fear, but hatred. "You think you've won?" Derek spat, his words slow and deliberate, like poison. "This is just the beginning. You'll never get rid of me."

Ethan didn't flinch. "You're not in control anymore. It's over."

For a moment, Derek simply glared at him, the fury in his eyes burning bright. Then, to Ethan's surprise, he started to laugh. It was a low, mirthless sound that echoed through the warehouse, and for a moment, Ethan couldn't tell if Derek was truly mad or if this was some kind of twisted game he was playing.

"You think I'm done?" Derek's voice was filled with venom. "You think you can just take control of everything I've built?"

Ethan's jaw tightened. "You never built anything. You manipulated people. You used them. And that's over."

Derek's laughter stopped abruptly, and the room seemed to fall into an unnatural silence. Ethan could hear his own heartbeat in his ears, feel the tension that stretched between them like a taut wire, ready to snap. Derek's eyes never left his, and for a brief second, Ethan had the unsettling feeling that Derek wasn't defeated. He wasn't giving up. He was waiting.

Suddenly, the door to the warehouse creaked open, and a figure stepped inside. The tall, imposing shape of Sheriff Collins filled the doorway, his hand hovering over the gun holstered at his side. The sheriff's face was unreadable, but there was no mistaking the way his eyes flicked over to Derek, then to Ethan, and finally to the wreckage around them.

"Collins," Derek said, his voice dripping with the remnants of his confidence. "I didn't expect you to show up."

The sheriff didn't respond immediately. Instead, he took a step closer, his eyes narrowing as they settled on Ethan. "What the hell's going on here?"

Ethan's mind raced, trying to piece together the situation. He couldn't trust the sheriff. Not now. Not after everything Lena had told him. But he had to play this carefully. One wrong move, and everything would fall apart.

"He tried to blow up the warehouse," Ethan said, his voice steady despite the adrenaline still coursing through his veins. "He was planning to destroy everything."

Collins didn't blink. He didn't even flinch. Instead, he looked over at Derek, who was still standing, his chest heaving with anger, but there was something in his eyes now—something like a man who knew the game was up.

"And you think you can stop me?" Derek sneered. "You think you've won, but you're too late. I've already set things in motion. You're just too blind to see it."

Ethan's heart skipped a beat. The implication was clear. Derek wasn't talking about this warehouse. He was talking about something much bigger—something far more dangerous.

"What are you talking about?" Ethan demanded, stepping forward. "What's your endgame, Derek?"

Derek's gaze flickered briefly toward Collins, then back to Ethan. For a brief moment, it looked like he might say something, but then he simply smirked, a twisted, self-satisfied smile. "You'll see," he said softly, his voice laced with cold certainty. "You'll all see. Sooner or later, you'll understand just how deep this runs."

Ethan's mind raced. What was Derek talking about? He knew there was more to this than the small-scale scheme he had tried to orchestrate in Willow Creek, but what did he mean by "soon"?

The sheriff cleared his throat, stepping forward, his gaze sharp as he regarded both men. "Enough of this." He didn't raise his voice, but there was an authority in his words. "You two are coming with me. Both of you."

Ethan's muscles tensed. This was it. The moment of truth.

But something about the way Collins spoke—the way his voice lingered just a fraction too long—set off alarm bells in Ethan's head. This wasn't a simple arrest. This wasn't just a sheriff doing his job. Collins had been in on it, hadn't he? He was part of this twisted web of lies. He'd always been loyal to Derek, and the idea that he would suddenly decide to turn on him didn't add up.

Ethan glanced over at Derek again, who was watching the exchange with a gleam of something like amusement.

"I wouldn't do that if I were you, Collins," Derek said, his voice laced with smugness.

The sheriff stiffened, and Ethan's instincts flared. Something was very wrong.

"What are you talking about?" Ethan demanded, his voice sharp as he took a step toward the sheriff, his mind racing. No. This wasn't happening.

And then, as if on cue, the sound of engines roared to life outside the warehouse. The unmistakable sound of more cars— more men—arriving.

Derek's smirk grew wider, almost gleeful, as he turned to face the sheriff. "You didn't really think you could walk away from this, did you?" His words were calm, almost friendly, but there was a dangerous edge to them.

Ethan's blood ran cold. He could see it now—the game Derek had been playing, the strings he had been pulling. The sheriff had been working with him all along. But it was more than that. It was a covert operation, and Derek wasn't just controlling Willow Creek—he was positioning himself as a power that spanned far beyond this small town. The sheriff was just one of many people Derek had in his pocket.

And now, as more black cars pulled into the yard, Ethan realized just how deeply entrenched Derek was. This was bigger than him, bigger than Lena, bigger than Willow Creek. It was bigger than all of them.

The sheriff moved toward Ethan slowly, a gun in his hand, his eyes never leaving him. "You don't understand, do you? You thought you could just come in here, stir things up, and walk away with a victory. You don't get to win this one, Cole. Not this time."

Ethan took a deep breath, his heart hammering in his chest. He knew this wasn't going to end with a simple fight. There were too many players, too many forces working against him. But he wasn't going to give up. Not now.

Not when the stakes were this high.

"You've made a mistake," Ethan said, his voice steady, despite the chaos unfolding around him. "This is over, Collins. You'll see that when the truth comes out."

The sheriff's face remained unreadable. He wasn't intimidated. But then, he wasn't expecting what happened next.

A figure appeared in the doorway—someone Ethan hadn't expected to see.

Lena.

She stood in the doorway, her eyes narrowed with resolve, her hands clenched into fists at her sides. The very air seemed to still as she stepped forward, her gaze locking with the sheriff's.

"Step aside, Collins," Lena said, her voice unwavering, filled with a quiet strength that sent a chill through the room. "You've already lost."

The sheriff hesitated. He had no idea what Lena had just done, what she had uncovered, or how deep Derek's corruption ran. But in that moment, it didn't matter. Everything had changed.

The game was over.

And the truth was about to come crashing down on Willow Creek.

Fifteen

Tipping the Scales

The atmosphere in the warehouse was electric, charged with the tension of a thousand unsaid words. Ethan stood at the center of it all, his body coiled tight, his mind racing with the consequences of what had just been revealed.

Lena was standing beside him, unwavering, her eyes locked on Sheriff Collins, who was now standing in front of them, looking more like a cornered animal than the man who had once exuded control. Behind him, the sound of more vehicles approaching sent a fresh wave of dread through Ethan's chest. It wasn't just Derek they had to worry about anymore; it was the entire system of corruption that had allowed him to operate unchecked for so long.

But Lena was ready.

"Step aside, Collins," Lena repeated, her voice steady, unyielding. It was a command, not a plea, and something in her tone made Ethan's breath catch. She had changed. She had grown into someone who would no longer allow herself to be controlled, someone who would no longer bow to the weight of fear.

Collins, still holding his gun with a practiced ease, didn't lower it. His eyes flicked between Lena and Ethan, his jaw clenched, but he didn't move a muscle. Instead, he raised his other hand slowly, almost as if to say he was in control, despite the fact that everyone in the room could feel the shifting of power.

"You have no idea what you're doing," Collins growled, his voice edged with panic that only now started to show through the cracks in his composure. "This goes beyond you, beyond both of you. This is bigger than the town. You can't stop it. No one can."

Ethan felt the surge of anger in his chest. How many lives had Collins ruined? How many people had he silenced just to keep his deals with Derek hidden from the world?

"We're not stopping anything, Collins," Ethan said coldly, his fists clenched at his sides. "We're exposing the truth."

The sheriff's eyes hardened. "You think the truth is enough to take me down? Do you think anyone will believe you? You're just one man with a vendetta. A man who doesn't know the first thing about how things work around here."

Ethan moved forward slowly, his gaze never leaving the sheriff's. The weight of his words hung heavy in the air, and he could see the shift in Collins' posture, the flicker of doubt behind his mask of confidence. The sheriff was realizing—the game was up.

Lena stepped forward, her presence steady beside Ethan. "It's not about one man, Collins. It's about everyone you've been using. Everyone you've hurt. And if you think you're going to walk away from this, you're wrong. You're going to answer for everything you've done."

Sheriff Collins' finger twitched on the trigger, but there was something in his eyes now—something close to fear. He wasn't used to feeling cornered, and he certainly wasn't used to being out of control. The fear radiating from him was almost palpable, and in that moment, Ethan knew that Collins wasn't the one in charge anymore.

The air seemed to grow thick with the weight of it all, like the very room was holding its breath.

And then, the unmistakable sound of car doors slamming shut reached their ears, followed by the quiet murmur of voices outside. Ethan didn't need to see who was approaching. He knew.

Derek's men were here.

There was a shift in the atmosphere, a new level of tension building in the warehouse. The air felt heavier now, like a storm was rolling in, waiting to break. The thudding of Ethan's heart became louder in his chest, and as the first of Derek's men stepped through the door, it was like time itself had slowed.

Three men entered, each of them built like a brick wall. They were dressed in black, their eyes hidden beneath dark glasses, their movements calculated and cold. They didn't speak, just moved to form a wall around Derek, who was now standing at the far side of the warehouse, his eyes cold and calculating. He didn't look at Ethan, didn't even spare him a glance. Instead, he looked to Lena, the malicious grin still in place.

"You think this is over, don't you?" Derek said softly, the sneer in his voice evident. "You think because you've disarmed my plans here, you've won? You think the people in this town will follow you? You're wrong."

Lena stepped forward, her eyes locked on Derek's. There was a calm in her now, a composure that Ethan hadn't seen before. She wasn't the girl who had been running anymore. She was the woman who had finally found her voice.

"Your time's up, Derek," she said, her voice steady. "The people in this town may have been afraid of you, but they're not anymore. You're not untouchable. This town belongs to them, not you."

Derek's eyes flicked to the sheriff, who was still holding his gun. The sheriff's face had paled, and for the first time, Derek seemed to realize that things weren't going to go the way he expected.

But the moment of uncertainty didn't last long. Derek's smile returned, though it was colder, sharper. "You're naïve, Lena. You really think you've won? That the people will turn against me?" He turned his gaze to the men behind him, his voice lowering, almost conspiratorial. "You think the mayor will side with you? Think again. He's already signed the papers. He's already agreed to everything."

Ethan stepped forward, cutting through the tension like a blade. "If the mayor is involved, then we'll make sure the truth comes out. You're not invincible, Derek. And neither is your little empire."

Derek's lips twisted into something between a grimace and a smile. "You really believe that, don't you? You're so sure of yourselves. But you're forgetting one thing." His eyes flashed with something dangerous. "The town is already mine."

Ethan froze. He could feel the weight of Derek's words, like a trap closing around them. What Derek was saying—it wasn't just about Willow Creek anymore. It was bigger. Derek had already made deals. This was more than just a small-time operation. This was a power grab that spanned every corner of the town—and beyond.

Lena's face paled as she caught the implication. "What do you mean?" she demanded. "What have you done?"

Derek's smile widened, his voice dripping with malice. "I've been preparing for this day. All my efforts weren't just about controlling Willow Creek. I have allies in the government. I've already arranged for a deal that will expand my influence far beyond this town. You're both too late to stop it."

Ethan's heart thudded in his chest. The realization hit him like a sledgehammer. Derek's plans were bigger than anyone had imagined. His influence reached further than the town. This was a larger operation, something that involved people outside of Willow Creek.

Lena stepped forward, her face twisted with anger. "You're lying. You can't have that kind of control. You can't…"

Derek interrupted her, his voice sharp, cutting through her words. "You think I don't have the resources? The connections? You think the mayor hasn't been in on this? I've been carefully positioning myself. And now I'm on the verge of taking everything. You'll see. The truth will be buried under layers of bureaucracy, and I will come out on top."

Ethan could feel the urgency in the air. This was more than a town. This was a network of people, of institutions, all wrapped up in a web of lies and corruption. And the truth—the real truth—was buried beneath all of it.

But they had to uncover it. They had to bring it all to light.

Ethan's gaze never left Derek as he turned toward Lena. "We're not giving up. Not now. Not ever."

Lena nodded, her expression fierce. "We'll take this to the people. To the press. To anyone who will listen. You can't hide behind your lies anymore, Derek."

Derek laughed, the sound bitter and mocking. "You think a few people with pitchforks will change anything? You think you'll win this, Lena? You've already lost."

Ethan stepped forward, his stance unwavering. "We haven't lost yet. But we will—if we let you keep talking."

He pulled the phone from his pocket and dialed quickly. A single call to someone who had the power to expose Derek's network, to make sure everything Derek had built came crashing down. He wasn't waiting any longer.

As the phone rang, Derek's eyes narrowed. He was cornered now, and it showed.

The call went through.

"This is Ethan Cole. I need to speak to someone who can make sure everything Derek's been hiding gets out there—now. Before it's too late."

The moment of silence that followed felt like an eternity. But as the line crackled with the voice on the other end, Ethan knew they were on the verge of ending this. The storm had arrived. And it was time for the reckoning.

Sixteen

The Final Hour

The room was suffocating. Every breath Ethan took felt heavy, laden with the weight of everything that had led to this moment. The phone call had been brief—too brief—but the voice on the other end had promised help, promised action. He couldn't afford to wait, though. They couldn't afford to be passive. Time was running out, and Derek was no longer the only threat in the room. There were others, others who had their fingers on the strings, pulling in ways Ethan and Lena hadn't even begun to understand.

Derek's men stood silently at the far side of the warehouse, like statues—unmoving, unreadable. Derek himself hadn't moved, hadn't shown any sign of fear or desperation. His eyes were locked on Ethan, full of contempt and the sort of confidence that comes with knowing you have the upper hand.

For now, at least.

Ethan was running out of patience. His fists clenched tightly at his sides, every muscle coiled, ready for the next move. He glanced over at Lena, who stood just a step behind him, her expression a mixture of resolve and fear. He could see the weariness in her eyes, the toll this had taken on her, and yet, there was something new there too. A fire. A strength that he hadn't seen in her before.

She wasn't the girl who had cowered in Derek's shadow anymore. She had become someone entirely different—someone who would fight for her town, for her future. And for herself.

Ethan's eyes flicked back to Derek, his mind sharpening, calculating the next move.

"You're still playing a game that's already over," Ethan said, his voice steady, but the tension underneath it was palpable. "You've been exposed, Derek. People are coming. You won't be able to hide behind your lies anymore."

Derek smiled, that same smug, dangerous smile that made Ethan want to punch him in the face. "You think this changes anything? You think the truth will matter when the pieces are already in place?"

The confidence in Derek's voice made Ethan's blood run cold. He knew Derek was dangerous, but this? This was something else. The whole town was about to be pulled under by Derek's grip, but Lena and Ethan still had one weapon they hadn't used yet. The truth. And they would see it out. No matter the cost.

Lena stepped forward now, her voice cool and cutting. "You've been lying to everyone, Derek. To me, to the town, to the people who trusted you. But I'm not going to let you do this anymore."

Derek's eyes shifted to her, something flickering behind his cold exterior—something like surprise, but quickly masked by a shadow of contempt.

"You think you can take me down with words?" Derek laughed, his voice echoing through the empty space of the warehouse. "You've been hiding for years, Lena. What makes you think you're suddenly a threat?"

Lena didn't flinch. She was done running. "Because I'm not hiding anymore. And neither are you."

The words hung in the air like a challenge, a promise. Derek's eyes narrowed, and for a moment, it felt like the world stopped. The fight was just beginning, and Lena wasn't backing down.

Ethan saw Derek's men shifting, the tension mounting. They could feel it too. The air was thick with impending action, and even though Derek was still standing tall, Ethan knew something had shifted. They were in the fight now, and no one was backing down.

A car door slammed outside, and for a moment, everyone in the room stilled. The sound of another vehicle rolling up sent a wave of anticipation through Ethan's veins. This was it. It was either now or never.

Derek's smirk widened, and he turned to his men. "You know what to do," he muttered, his voice barely audible over the din of the engines outside.

One of the men, tall and broad-shouldered, made a move toward the back of the warehouse, his footsteps heavy against the concrete floor. It was a distraction—Ethan could feel it. Derek was trying to move his men into position while he dealt with them. But Lena wasn't blind. She saw it, too.

Without thinking, she rushed forward, slamming her shoulder into one of Derek's men as he passed by. The man grunted in surprise but quickly recovered, reaching for his weapon.

Lena was faster.

She grabbed a loose metal rod from a nearby stack of crates and swung it hard, knocking the man off balance. He staggered back, but before he could regain his footing, Ethan was on him, a fist to his gut that left him gasping for air. The man crumpled to the ground in a heap.

Derek's eyes widened in surprise as his men struggled to keep up with the sudden shift in the situation. But there was no time to waste. The rest of Derek's men started to move, but Lena was already pushing forward, eyes locked on Derek, fury lighting her face.

"You're finished," Lena spat, her voice laced with determination.

Derek stepped back, his hand resting on the small of his back, fingers brushing the outline of a gun. "You're making a huge mistake."

Ethan advanced quickly, his eyes never leaving Derek's, moving between him and the remaining men. He could feel the air around him crackling, charged with the energy of an inevitable showdown.

But then, everything seemed to slow. There was a sudden loud crack as the wooden floorboards shifted, and just as Derek's hand reached the handle of his weapon, a voice cut through the tension.

"Stop right there."

The voice was calm but commanding. Familiar. Ethan's head snapped around, his body on high alert. He knew that voice.

The figure who stepped through the doorway wasn't who Ethan expected. It wasn't the police. It wasn't anyone from outside the town.

It was Sheriff Collins.

But this wasn't the same Collins who had been working for Derek. This was a man who looked exhausted, his face pale with guilt, his eyes filled with something like regret. His hand was raised, not holding a gun, but a badge.

"Collins?" Lena's voice was a whisper, barely audible over the rising tension. Her eyes searched his face, her heart beating faster in her chest. "What are you doing here?"

The sheriff looked at them, his gaze flicking nervously between the two of them and Derek, whose posture was now frozen, his earlier confidence slipping into something far more dangerous. He didn't know how this was going to play out, but his choice was clear.

"I… I couldn't let it happen anymore," Sheriff Collins said, his voice shaking. "I couldn't keep hiding behind Derek's lies. I've been a part of something wrong. And I don't want to be anymore."

Ethan's heart raced as he processed the words. Was this a trick? Was Collins trying to set them up? But the sheriff's eyes were sincere—his shoulders sagging with a weariness that spoke of too many years spent complicit in Derek's manipulation.

"I've been looking the other way for years," Collins continued, stepping closer, his badge catching the dim light. "But I can't do that anymore. I was a part of his plans, too. But not anymore."

Derek's laugh was short, devoid of humor. "You think they'll believe you, Collins? You think anyone cares what a coward like you has to say now?"

Collins didn't flinch. He met Derek's gaze squarely. "I'm not the one they'll listen to, Derek. It's over. You lost. And you won't walk away from this."

The finality in Collins's voice was unmistakable. The door had closed for Derek, and for the first time, the criminal was no longer in control. Ethan moved forward, pulling out his phone, ready to dial the authorities again. This time, they wouldn't be able to ignore what was happening in Willow Creek.

As the sirens grew louder in the distance, Derek's smirk faded, replaced by a look of bitter realization. He wasn't going to get away with it this time.

It was over. The web of lies, the manipulation, the fear. It was finally all coming to an end.

But as Derek's gaze flicked toward the exit, a new fire ignited in his eyes. He wasn't going to go down without a fight.

And neither was Ethan.

The moment was stretching toward something inevitable, the tension about to snap like the strings of a broken bow. This wasn't the end—not yet. It was the reckoning.

And everything was about to change.

Seventeen

The Last Stand

The sirens were louder now. The sound of them reverberated through the warehouse, blending with the oppressive silence that filled the room. The tension was palpable. It was as if the very air in the space had grown thick, heavy with the weight of everything that had happened—and everything that was about to unfold.

Ethan stood at the center of the room, his gaze never leaving Derek, who was now standing motionless, his hands clenched into fists. Derek's men had been subdued, their weapons disarmed, but the man himself hadn't moved. His face was a mask of fury and disbelief, but beneath it all, there was something else—something that Ethan could almost feel, a kind of cold calculation, the last remnants of his twisted confidence.

And then there was the sheriff—Collins—still standing by the door, his eyes flicking between the two of them, his hand still hovering near his sidearm. Lena stood beside Ethan, her presence a solid anchor in the storm. She wasn't the same woman who had been cowering in fear before Derek, and Ethan could see the strength radiating from her, the way she held herself now, unafraid. They were facing Derek, but they were no longer alone. This time, they had the truth.

Derek's eyes narrowed as he sized up the situation. "You really think this is it, don't you?" he sneered, his voice dripping with venom. "You think you can just walk in here and destroy everything I've built? Do you really believe it's that simple?"

Ethan didn't flinch. He wasn't intimidated anymore. The game had changed. "It's not about destroying it, Derek," he said, his voice steady and sure. "It's about exposing you for what you really are."

Derek's lips curled into a bitter smile. "Expose me? What a joke. You have no idea what you're up against." He paused, letting the words hang in the air like a taunt. "You think you've taken everything from me, but you're just a pawn in a much bigger game. You've never even seen the full picture."

Lena's hand found Ethan's, her grip firm, but her voice was cold as she spoke. "I don't care about your game anymore. You're done, Derek. People are going to know what you've done. And you're not going to get away with it."

For a moment, the room was still, the only sound the distant hum of the approaching sirens. Derek took a slow step forward, his eyes burning with hatred, but Ethan didn't back away. This was it. The final confrontation. There was no turning back now.

"You don't understand," Derek said, his voice lowering. "I've got people in places you wouldn't even dream of. You're not going to take me down, not when I have the mayor, the sheriff, and half the town on my side." He looked at Collins, his eyes almost pleading. "Collins, you know this isn't how it's supposed to go. We're too far along. You can't just walk away."

Collins's face remained unreadable, but his hand was still near his gun. He didn't speak, but his posture—stiff, tense—said it all. For the first time, the sheriff wasn't sure which side he was on.

Ethan's pulse quickened. He could feel the shift in the air—the way everything seemed to pause for a heartbeat, as if the room was waiting for something, waiting for someone to make the next move. And then, before anyone could say another word, the door at the back of the warehouse slammed open.

The unexpected noise jolted everyone to attention, and the figure who stepped into the room was like a ghost materializing from the shadows.

It was Mayor Whitfield.

Ethan's breath caught in his throat. The mayor, the very man who had been part of Derek's schemes, had walked right into the middle of everything. His expression was cold, calculating, the same man who had dealt with the corrupt system that had allowed Derek to thrive for so long.

Ethan knew then—this was the last piece of the puzzle. This was the man who had been feeding Derek all the power he had, the man who had allowed him to control the town, to manipulate everyone in his path.

"Whitfield," Derek said, his voice tinged with relief, as though his arrival signified something. "I was wondering when you'd show up."

The mayor looked past Derek, his eyes locking with Ethan's, then with Lena's. There was no sign of fear in his gaze. Instead, it was something colder, something more dangerous. He didn't look like a man caught in a trap—he looked like a man who had already made his move.

"You think this ends here?" Whitfield asked, his voice a quiet, controlled threat. "You think you can come into this town and tear it all apart? You don't know who you're dealing with."

Ethan took a deep breath, stepping forward, keeping his voice calm but unwavering. "You've been hiding behind Derek this whole time, haven't you, Whitfield? You've been using him to keep your hands clean, but it's over now. The people are going to know what you've done."

The mayor smirked, the arrogance on his face unmistakable. "You really believe that? The truth doesn't matter here, Ethan. Not anymore. The people will never side with you. They need someone like me. Someone who keeps the wheels turning." He glanced at Derek, who stood beside him, the two of them a pair of criminals too deeply embedded in the town's infrastructure to be dislodged. "You don't understand how this works. It's bigger than you."

Lena's voice broke through the heavy silence. "No, it's not bigger than us. It's bigger than you." She took a step forward, her voice rising with intensity. "The people will stand with us. We'll expose everything, and the truth will come out. You've been lying to everyone for so long, and this—" she pointed to the sheriff, to Derek, and finally to the mayor, "—is the moment when it all falls apart. The truth always comes out in the end."

Whitfield's smile faded slightly, but he didn't show any signs of backing down. "Do you think you can just bring the town to its knees? You think the people will turn against me and Derek just because you say so?"

The sound of distant sirens became deafening, filling the air like an impending storm. And that was when Ethan realized something—something that sent a cold shiver down his spine. The truth wouldn't be enough to save them.

They needed more than just words. They needed something that could break the entire system apart, something that could make even Whitfield and Derek see that their time was over.

"Not just because I say so," Ethan replied, his voice low but filled with purpose. "Because I've got proof. I've got the evidence you've been hiding all these years. And I'm going to make sure everyone knows who you really are."

Ethan turned to Collins, his voice steady. "You're not getting away with this. Not after everything."

For a split second, it looked like the sheriff was going to speak, but the words never came. Instead, his hand slowly dropped from his gun, his fingers trembling slightly. The expression on his face shifted—hesitation, uncertainty. He looked at Derek, then at the mayor, and then back at Ethan and Lena, the weight of his decision hanging heavily in the air.

"I..." Collins began, his voice wavering. "I can't protect you anymore, Derek. I can't protect any of this." His eyes flicked to the mayor, and for the first time, Ethan saw the sheriff's resolve fracture. "I'm done."

Derek's eyes narrowed, his lips curling into a sneer. "You're a fool," he spat. But there was no real venom in his words, just panic. He knew that the game was slipping through his fingers.

The mayor stepped forward, a dark look crossing his face. "You'll regret this," Whitfield said, his voice low and threatening. But there was a trace of fear in his eyes now—real fear. The walls were closing in.

Ethan didn't wait for him to say anything more. "We're not afraid of you anymore, Whitfield. You've lost."

The sirens grew louder, closer now. It wouldn't be long before the authorities arrived to take over, to take down the people who had controlled this town for so long.

But as Derek and the mayor exchanged one last look, Ethan realized that this wasn't just about them anymore. This wasn't about Derek or Whitfield. It was about the people of Willow Creek. It was about their future, and about finally taking the power back.

The moment of truth was here. The reckoning had arrived.

And there was no going back.

Eighteen

The Final Hour

The sirens were deafening now, the sounds of multiple cruisers and emergency vehicles echoing through the narrow streets of Willow Creek, growing louder with every passing second. The tension in the warehouse was palpable, thick enough to cut with a knife. Derek, the mayor, and the sheriff were still in their positions—cornered and visibly shaken, but they hadn't yet given up. Lena stood next to Ethan, her hands clenched tightly at her sides, her gaze unwavering as she watched the three men who had thought they controlled everything.

The truth had begun to unravel, and there was no escaping it now. But as the sound of the approaching police cars grew louder, Ethan knew they were entering the final stretch. What happened next would determine the fate of Willow Creek—and possibly, the people who had been living in its shadow for so long.

Derek had lost his composure, and the smirk that had once been so sure of itself now looked like the mask of a desperate man. His eyes flicked between the sheriff, the mayor, and Ethan, the weight of realization sinking in. His empire, built on lies, manipulation, and fear, was collapsing.

The mayor stood slightly apart from the group, his face pale but still holding onto the arrogance that had defined him for so long. He wasn't giving up, not without a fight. The sheriff, on the other hand, had dropped his hand from his holster and was standing to the side, his face drawn with guilt.

Ethan could see the change in Collins. The sheriff, once so loyal to Derek, was now questioning everything. The way he looked at Derek—there was no doubt left in his eyes. He had already made his choice.

Lena's voice cut through the silence, steady but full of force. "This ends tonight, Derek. There's no going back now."

Derek's eyes snapped to her, his expression darkening with a mixture of disbelief and fury. "You think this is over? You think I'm just going to let you and your little friend come in here and tear everything down? You don't know what's at stake."

"You're right," Lena replied, her voice as sharp as a blade. "I don't know what you've done. But I know it's over. The town is tired of being afraid of you."

Derek's gaze flicked toward Collins, then to the mayor, seeking an ally in the room, but there was none. The sheriff had already betrayed him, and the mayor—though still standing tall—had no more cards to play. They were all too deep in the muck of this town's corruption to back out now. The walls were closing in, and there was nothing Derek could do to stop it.

"You've already lost," Lena continued, her voice unwavering. "People are coming. The truth is coming."

Derek's jaw tightened. "You think I'm the only one who's controlled this town, huh? You think the mayor's any better than me? You think he's not just as guilty?" He turned toward Whitfield, his voice a mocking growl. "You think anyone's going to believe you now?"

Whitfield's lips curled into a thin smile, but his eyes were nervous, flicking toward the door, listening to the sound of approaching sirens. He knew it was over, but he wasn't willing to give up without a final stand. His arrogance hadn't entirely shattered. "You're both fools," the mayor said, his voice tight, struggling to maintain some shred of authority. "You think you've won? You don't have the power to stop what's coming."

The tension in the room was unbearable. Every second that passed brought the arrival of the authorities closer, and every word spoken felt like the final countdown.

Ethan's pulse quickened as he stepped closer to the mayor. "You think the people will side with you?" he asked, his voice low but filled with disgust. "After everything you've done? After the lies you've fed them? You're done, Whitfield. You're going to be held accountable. All of you are."

Derek's men, still standing at the back of the room, seemed to sense that something was shifting. The air was thick with anticipation, but they didn't move, waiting for a sign that it was time to act. They were still loyal, but even they knew the battle was over. No one had expected the sheriff to turn, no one had seen it coming. But now, the realization was dawning on them that Derek was the last one standing—and he was no longer the leader he'd once been.

"You can't save yourselves anymore," Lena said, stepping forward. "We have the evidence. We have everything we need to take you down."

Derek took a step back, his eyes scanning the room like a trapped animal, seeking an escape, a way out of the hole he'd dug himself into. He had always been a man of action, never one to stand still for long. But now, he was cornered—caught in a web of lies, with no way to crawl out. His empire was crumbling around him, and all he had left was his stubborn pride.

"You don't understand, do you?" Derek hissed, his voice growing more frantic by the second. "You think this is the end? That exposing me will solve everything? You don't know the half of it. You don't know who you're dealing with."

Lena's face hardened. "I don't need to know everything. I just need to know that it's over. You don't control this town anymore."

Derek's face twisted with rage, his eyes flashing with a wild, dangerous gleam. His hand shot out toward his jacket, but before he could reach for a weapon, Ethan was already moving.

In one fluid motion, Ethan rushed toward Derek, knocking his arm away before he could grab his gun. The two collided, Derek's body slamming against a stack of crates as Ethan pressed him to the ground. Derek struggled, thrashing beneath him, but Ethan had him pinned, his body weight keeping him immobilized.

"You've had your chance, Derek," Ethan said, his voice cold, his grip tightening. "Now it's over."

Derek snarled beneath him. "You can't keep me here forever, Cole. You think you've won, but you haven't seen the worst of it. I have connections, people who will make sure this town stays mine. You think you're the hero? You think anyone will believe you?"

Ethan didn't respond. He didn't need to. He was done talking.

From the corner of the room, Lena stepped forward, holding up a flash drive, her eyes locked on Derek. "We've got everything we need," she said. "Every piece of evidence, every lie you've told, every deal you've made with the mayor, the sheriff, and your men. It's all here. We're going to take this to the press. To the authorities. And you're going to be exposed for everything you are."

Derek's expression flickered with disbelief, then twisted into something darker. He struggled against Ethan's grip, but Ethan held firm, pinning him to the ground. There was no way out for Derek now. His empire was destroyed, and there was no escaping the truth that had finally caught up with him.

The sirens outside grew louder, and then the sound of heavy boots hitting the concrete floor reached their ears. The police had arrived.

Ethan didn't release Derek immediately. He could feel the man's rage beneath him, the way Derek's body tensed as though he was preparing to make a final, desperate move. But Ethan didn't flinch. He was ready for this.

The doors to the warehouse burst open, and the first officers poured into the room, weapons drawn. They took in the scene quickly—Ethan on top of Derek, Lena holding up the evidence, Collins standing at the back of the room, his face a mixture of guilt and uncertainty.

One of the officers shouted for Derek to freeze, but Derek didn't listen. Instead, he lunged toward the nearest officer, but before he could reach him, Ethan shoved him back to the ground with a force that knocked the wind out of him.

"He's not going anywhere," Ethan snapped, his voice fierce. "You don't have to worry about him anymore."

The officers quickly moved in, handcuffing Derek and pulling him away from Ethan. As they dragged him to his feet, Derek continued to struggle, thrashing against them, his eyes wild with frustration.

"You think this is over?" he spat. "You think you've won?"

Ethan looked at him, his voice cold and final. "Yes, Derek. We've won."

As the officers took Derek away, the tension in the room finally began to ease. The weight that had hung in the air for so long—the fear, the uncertainty, the lies—was finally dissipating. The truth was out. Derek and the mayor had been exposed. The town would never be the same. And neither would Ethan or Lena.

Ethan turned to Lena, his heart swelling with a mix of relief and exhaustion. She had fought so hard, just as he had. Together, they had taken down the system of fear and control that had plagued this town for far too long.

The sirens outside were finally silenced, but the sound of the officers moving through the warehouse was a reminder of the work that was still to be done. There were more people to arrest, more people to expose, and more lies to unravel. But for the first time in a long while, Willow Creek had a chance at something different.

Ethan stepped closer to Lena, his voice soft but full of resolve. "It's over. We did it."

Lena's eyes met his, and for the first time in a long while, she smiled—a smile that was free of fear. The weight of the past was still there, but it no longer held her captive. Together, they had taken the first step toward a new beginning.

And for the first time, they were both free.

Nineteen

Aftermath

The sound of police radios crackled through the air, cutting through the tense silence that had settled over the warehouse. The officers were everywhere, working quickly, securing the area, taking statements, arresting Derek's men, and collecting the evidence that would expose everything. But to Ethan, it felt like the world had come to a standstill. Every movement around him seemed distant, as though he was seeing the world through a fog. It wasn't relief that filled him; it was something heavier.

They had won. Derek had been arrested. The truth was out. But that victory—though hard-earned—came at a cost.

Ethan glanced at Lena, standing beside him, her face a mask of exhaustion and disbelief. Her eyes were fixed on the officers, her jaw clenched tightly, but there was something else there too—something like a quiet resolve. It was over, but it was only the beginning.

The two of them had been through so much in the last few days. There was so much to process—so much that neither of them had been able to truly comprehend until now. They had both fought for this moment, for freedom from Derek's clutches, and now that it was here, there was a feeling of emptiness, like the weight of the world had suddenly lifted off their shoulders, leaving them hollow.

"Is it over?" Lena's voice broke through the stillness, quiet but raw, like she was trying to make sense of it all.

Ethan turned to her, his gaze meeting hers. There were no words to describe how he felt, no easy answers to offer. But he could see it in her eyes—the same confusion, the same weight of what had just happened.

"It's over," he said softly, the words not quite carrying the finality he wanted them to. "But we still have to deal with the fallout."

Lena nodded slowly, her eyes flicking back to the group of officers who were now escorting Derek out of the warehouse in handcuffs. Derek, the man who had once controlled everything—who had ruled with fear and manipulation—was now a broken shell, dragged away in shame. Ethan should've felt satisfied. He should've felt a sense of accomplishment. But all he could think about was how much it had cost. How many lives had been ruined? How many people had fallen under Derek's influence without even knowing?

"What happens now?" Lena asked, her voice so quiet that Ethan almost didn't hear her.

"I don't know," he admitted. "We tell the truth. We make sure everyone knows what happened. We make sure Derek can't hurt anyone again. But the town? It won't be easy. People will question everything. They'll wonder how they could have missed it."

Lena's gaze remained fixed on the officers, her brow furrowed. "I don't know if I'll ever be able to trust them again."

The weight of her words sank into Ethan's chest like a stone. She was right. The truth had come out, but the lies had been so deeply embedded in Willow Creek's fabric that it was hard to imagine the town ever being the same. So many had turned a blind eye to the corruption, to the things they had known but chosen to ignore.

Ethan stepped closer to Lena, his hand brushing against hers, offering her some measure of comfort. They were in this together, and even though the road ahead was uncertain, they would face it side by side.

"They'll have to change," Ethan said, his voice low but firm. "People will have to look at this town differently. They'll have to hold each other accountable."

Lena nodded, but her gaze was distant. "I don't know if I can ever trust this place again."

"You don't have to," Ethan replied, his voice steady. "You don't have to trust anyone but yourself. You've done what you needed to do. You've freed yourself. And now you can start over."

For a moment, Lena didn't respond. She just stared at the officers, her expression unreadable, as if lost in her thoughts. Ethan could feel the weight of the moment pressing down on him. They had both fought so hard to get here, and now that they had arrived, the future felt uncertain. They had exposed Derek's crimes, but would the town ever truly change? Could it ever be the place they both wanted it to be?

Ethan let out a long breath, his mind shifting back to the task at hand. There was still much to do. They needed to make sure the evidence was passed on to the right people—officials who could prosecute Derek and everyone who had been involved in his schemes. But there was more. Much more. The town was broken, and it wasn't going to heal overnight.

"I'm not going anywhere," Ethan said finally, breaking the silence between them. He turned to Lena, his eyes meeting hers with conviction. "We'll make sure this doesn't happen again. We'll rebuild Willow Creek."

Lena turned her head toward him, her eyes searching his face, as though looking for some sort of confirmation. She didn't respond immediately, but after a moment, she nodded slowly. "I don't want to leave," she said softly. "This is my home. I've spent so many years trying to escape, but… maybe this is where I'm meant to be. Maybe this is where I can finally start over."

Ethan smiled, a small but genuine expression that made something in his chest relax. "Then we'll rebuild it together. We'll make it a place worth fighting for."

Before Lena could respond, the sound of footsteps interrupted their conversation. Ethan turned to see an officer walking toward them, his face stern. "Mr. Cole, Miss Parker," the officer said, his tone respectful but urgent. "We need to speak with both of you."

Ethan and Lena exchanged a glance before following the officer. The reality of their situation was finally settling in. The truth was out. But the consequences of that truth were only beginning.

The officer led them to a small room at the back of the warehouse, a simple space with a table in the center. He gestured for them to sit, and once they did, he took a seat across from them. He didn't waste any time.

"I know this has been difficult, but we need your cooperation," the officer began, his eyes flicking between the two of them. "We've got the evidence we need to press charges against Derek, the mayor, and the others. But we still need statements from both of you. We need the details, everything you've uncovered, so we can build the case."

Ethan exhaled slowly, feeling the weight of what was to come. He looked over at Lena, who was nodding, her expression grim but determined.

"We'll help however we can," Lena said, her voice steady. "We'll make sure this doesn't happen again."

The officer nodded, and for a brief moment, there was a look of respect in his eyes. "Good. Because this town needs to hear your story. The truth needs to come out. And we'll make sure it does."

Ethan sat back in his chair, his mind still racing, his thoughts flicking between the conversation at hand and the overwhelming reality of what had just happened. They were about to take down the power structure of an entire town, to expose the lies and corruption that had festered for so long. The truth would break it all apart—but would it be enough to heal the wounds?

It was hard to imagine Willow Creek ever being the same again. There was so much that had been lost—so much damage had been done—but Ethan could feel something stirring in him, a glimmer of hope, as if, just maybe, there was a way forward.

The officer's voice broke through his thoughts. "We'll need a detailed account of everything—of Derek's involvement, the mayor's actions, and everything you both uncovered. The sooner we have it, the sooner we can move forward."

Ethan nodded slowly, his mind focused. "We'll give you everything. Everything you need."

As the officer stood and left the room to gather the paperwork, Lena turned to Ethan, her expression more serious than he had ever seen it.

"We can't let this happen again," she said quietly, her voice thick with emotion. "Not to anyone. We have to make sure this town knows the truth."

Ethan's heart swelled, and he reached out to take her hand, holding it firmly. "We will," he promised. "We'll make sure they do."

Outside the room, the officers were still working, moving swiftly and with purpose. The air was thick with the tension of a battle just won but not over. They had broken Derek's grip on the town, but the real work was just beginning. They had to rebuild, to make sure the cycle of fear and corruption never took root again.

Ethan didn't know what the future held, but he knew one thing for sure. Whatever came next, he and Lena would face it together. The town might have been broken, but it wasn't beyond saving. Not if they had anything to say about it.

And together, they would fight for it.

Twenty

New Beginnings

The days following Derek's arrest passed in a blur of police interrogations, statements, and endless paperwork. The town of Willow Creek was slowly coming to terms with the truth, the rot that had seeped through its bones for years. The mayor's involvement, the sheriff's complicity, and Derek's web of manipulation had all been laid bare, and now it was up to the people to rebuild from the ashes.

But as the dust settled, Ethan couldn't shake the feeling that this wasn't truly over. Something was unfinished in the air, lingering in the town like an unspoken promise. Derek had been taken down, yes. But the damage he'd caused was deep, and it wasn't just the people who had been directly involved that were left to pick up the pieces—it was the town itself. The systems of power that had been put in place, the networks of corruption, would take more than just a few arrests to dismantle.

Ethan sat at the kitchen table, staring out the window at the quiet streets of Willow Creek. The sun was setting, casting long shadows over the sleepy town, and for the first time in a long while, the air felt still. Peaceful. But he knew it was only temporary. There was still so much work to be done, and the road ahead wouldn't be easy.

Lena entered the room, her footsteps soft, but Ethan could feel her presence even before she spoke. She moved to the counter, her fingers absentmindedly tracing the rim of a coffee mug, her expression distant. She hadn't said much in the past few days. The weight of everything—of what they'd uncovered, of what had been lost—seemed to have settled heavily on her shoulders.

"You okay?" Ethan asked, breaking the silence.

Lena turned toward him, her eyes meeting his with a small, tired smile. "I'm not sure what 'okay' even means anymore." She exhaled slowly, walking over to join him at the table. "It's strange, you know? I never thought we'd make it this far. That we'd actually expose everything. It feels... surreal."

Ethan nodded, understanding exactly what she meant. It was hard to grasp the enormity of it all—the fact that they had finally exposed the corruption that had been controlling the town for so long. But even now, in the quiet aftermath, he couldn't shake the feeling that something was still looming over them. He hadn't been able to put it into words, but there was a gnawing sense of unease in his gut, like there was more to the story, more they hadn't yet uncovered.

"Do you ever think about what comes next?" Lena asked, her voice quiet.

Ethan glanced at her, his heart heavy with the question. "What do you mean?"

"I mean, we've taken down Derek. We've exposed everything, but now what?" Her eyes seemed to search his, looking for the answer he didn't have. "The people, the town—they're still broken. The damage is done, and even though Derek is behind bars, it doesn't feel like enough. There's more to fix."

Ethan leaned back in his chair, his fingers tapping on the wooden surface. He hadn't really thought about it, not in any tangible way. He'd been so focused on the immediate danger—on taking Derek down—that he hadn't stopped to think about what came after. He hadn't thought about the rebuilding process, the work it would take to heal the town, to give people the hope they had lost.

"You're right," he said finally, his voice quieter now. "It's not just about arresting Derek. It's about what we do next. We need to make sure this never happens again. We need to change things from the ground up."

Lena nodded, her expression thoughtful. "It's not going to be easy. People are going to fight it. There are going to be people who want to hold onto the old way of things—people who are afraid of what will happen if we tear it all down."

Ethan stood up, moving toward the window and looking out at the darkening street. The houses across the way were quiet, but he knew that there were conversations happening behind those closed doors, conversations about the future of the town. Some people would want to go back to the way things were, to forget what had happened and pretend like nothing had changed. Others, like Lena and him, would have to fight to ensure that the truth was never buried again.

"We have to be the ones to lead that change," Ethan said, turning back toward her. "We can't wait for the town to fix itself. We need to start now. We need to show people that they can stand up, that they can be part of the solution."

Lena walked over to where he stood, standing close enough that he could feel the warmth of her presence. She reached out, her hand finding his, squeezing it gently. "I don't know where to start," she admitted, her voice small, almost uncertain. "I don't know how to fix all of this."

"You don't have to do it alone," Ethan replied, squeezing her hand in return. "We'll do it together. One step at a time. We'll show them what's possible."

The sound of a car pulling into the driveway interrupted the moment. Ethan looked out the window again, his gaze sharp, instinctively on alert. The car was unfamiliar, its headlights cutting through the darkness. The engine cut off, and then the sound of footsteps echoed on the porch.

Lena's hand slipped from his, and she moved to the window, peering out cautiously. "Who is that?"

Ethan frowned, his pulse quickening. "I don't know."

Before he could make a move to answer the door, the knock came.

Lena froze, her eyes flicking to Ethan. "Are you expecting anyone?"

"No." Ethan's voice was low, steady. He knew who it wasn't—Derek was locked away. The police had taken care of everything on that front. This wasn't a friendly visit. Something in his gut told him that.

Ethan walked toward the door, his mind racing as he opened it slowly, his hand lingering just above the handle of the gun he kept tucked under his jacket. He wasn't sure why, but he felt like this was the kind of moment where instinct would have to guide him.

Standing on the porch was a man he didn't recognize—tall, wearing a long black coat, and a fedora. His face was shadowed by the dim porch light, but Ethan could see enough to know that the man was older, maybe in his mid-fifties, with a sharp, calculated expression.

"Can I help you?" Ethan asked, keeping his voice neutral, his body angled just enough to protect Lena behind him.

The man smiled—a thin, tight-lipped smile—and his eyes glinted with something cold. "I'm here about your friend Derek."

Ethan's stomach clenched at the mention of Derek's name. Friend? This man didn't look like anyone who should have been in Derek's corner.

"I don't know what you're talking about," Ethan replied, his tone even, but his mind racing.

The man took a step closer, his gaze unwavering. "I think you do. You see, Mr. Cole, this town has been controlled for a long time, longer than you might think. Derek was just a piece of the puzzle. But you've already exposed him. Now, you're coming for the rest."

Ethan's breath caught. He couldn't stop himself from taking a small step back. He knew what was happening now. This wasn't over. There were still players behind the scenes, still people pulling strings in the darkness.

The man's voice lowered, becoming more insidious. "The truth doesn't always set you free, Ethan. Sometimes it just buries you deeper."

Ethan's mind spun. There were still more to expose? Still more hidden in the shadows? He had thought that with Derek's arrest, with the evidence in hand, everything would fall into place. But this man—this threat—had just proven him wrong.

Lena moved to stand beside Ethan, her eyes wide but determined. "Who are you?" she demanded, her voice sharp with accusation.

The man didn't answer at first. Instead, he took a step closer, his smile never wavering. "You'll find out soon enough," he said, his voice laced with a venomous calm.

Before Ethan could react, the man turned and walked back toward his car, his figure disappearing into the night like a shadow.

Lena's breath was shallow, her hand gripping Ethan's arm as she turned to face him. "What was that? Who was he?"

Ethan shook his head, a cold chill crawling up his spine. "I don't know. But it's clear now—this is just the beginning. We're not done yet."

As the man's car pulled away, disappearing into the darkened streets, Ethan knew one thing for certain. Derek wasn't the end of this fight. It was only the beginning.